LITTLE VICTORIES

LITTLE VICTORIES

PERFECT RULES

FOR IMPERFECT LIVING

JASON GAY

DOUBLEDAY

NEW YORK LONDON TORONTO

SYDNEY AUCKLAND

www.doubleday.com

DOUBLEDAY and the portrayal of an anchor with a dolphin
are registered trademarks of Penguin Random House LLC.

Jacket design by Janet Hansen

LIBRARY OF CONGRESS CATALOGING-IN-PUBLICATION DATA
Gay, Jason (Newspaper columnist)
Little victories : perfect rules for imperfect living /
Jason Gay. — First Edition.
pages cm
ISBN 978-0-385-53946-3 (hardcover)
ISBN 978-0-385-53947-0 (eBook)
1. Self-actualization (Psychology) 2. Happiness. I. Title.
BF637.S4G3949 2015
650.1—dc23
2015009123

MANUFACTURED IN THE UNITED STATES OF AMERICA

First Edition

For Bessie

Contents

LITTLE VICTORIES

Little Victories

This was not long ago: I was back home, in Massachusetts, in the house I grew up in, sitting in the same kitchen I'd sat in my entire childhood and adolescence, eating . . . I have no idea what I was eating. Probably peanut butter. Random refrigerator finds dipped in peanut butter. It was very late, close to two in the morning. My mother was asleep. My father was asleep. I'd just come from work, if you could call it "work," because I had been about fifteen minutes away, covering the World Series as a sports columnist, which is about as stupid lucky a job as you can have, the kind of job that makes you think one day a stern-faced man with a clipboard is going to show up and say, *There was a terrible mistake. This isn't your job. You're supposed to be managing a karaoke bar for dogs.* In the morning I had to fly back to New York City, and I knew that upon waking, I would bicker with my dad about what time we needed to leave the house. This was always a comical argument, our version of Abbott and Costello. With no traffic, you can get from our house to the airport in a half hour. I believe leaving ninety minutes in advance is reasonable. My father preferred to leave in 1987.

In the darkness the kitchen looked so small. Let me be the ten thousandth person to point out that the house you grew up in does not resemble the house you visit as an adult. Its scale is lost, its proportions change, and the artifacts of your childhood have been rearranged or have vanished altogether. That woolly couch, the one with the painful buttons on the back ... where did that couch go? New discoveries reveal exotic, previously unknown details about your parents. There is truffle oil in the cabinet. *Truffle oil.* When did Mom and Dad start liking truffle oil? It's like finding a koala bear pawing around in the garage.

I went upstairs to my room, which hadn't been my room for more than two decades, and really was never fully mine, because for most of my childhood I shared it with my brother and a series of uncooperative cats. Privacy existed only in my thoughts. I knew this room to be the room where I became myself, or had fantasies of future selves that would never happen. This is the room where I wanted to be Larry Bird. Where I wanted to be Prince. Where I wanted to be Sting. (Yes, I wanted to be Sting. I'll come down and fight you right now.) It was the room where homework was done, or homework was not done, where girls were called and the fathers of girls were hung up on. This was the room where I found out a kid I knew from school, a teammate, had been killed in a car accident, the first moment I truly felt impermanent. This was the room where I learned I'd gotten rejected by a college. This was the room where I got rejected by another college. Then another college. I got rejected by a lot of colleges.

Things improved. I left this room and snuck into a school (thank you, sleepy admissions officer at the University of Wisconsin–Madison!) and found a job and experienced love and heartbreak and finally met the woman I would marry, Bessie. I'd gotten sick with cancer and recovered to the point that I'd forgotten it happened. I'd been blessed to get work that let me fly around the world and meet people I'd never dreamed of meeting and a handful of schnooks I hoped never to meet again. I'd been dispatched to Super Bowls, Summer and Winter Olympics, World Cups, and the snooty-pants golf Masters. If you're not impressed by any of that, I once saw a photograph of a bird on top of a mouse on top of a cat on top of a dog.

I sat awake in that room and all of that backstory rushed over me. I had been so happy and so unhappy here. But in the moment I mostly felt fortunate, to have lived here, in this house, in this town, with this family and these parents, and tried to think of all the things that had influenced me along the way. Sometimes it's easier just to believe that life's path is chance, a fluke of randomness, and yet it's not really random, not when you think about what you are and what you wanted to be and all the miles in between. And I thought about all the people who had imparted advice to me—good advice, bad advice, in and outside my family. I'd had plenty of mentors—mentors I sought, ones I didn't. Good bosses, jerk bosses. Great coaches, ambivalent coaches. You think you are on your own, but you really are not. Nobody figures it out alone.

I have my own children now. As I write this, my son, Jesse, is two years old; my daughter, Josie, is a happy, hungry newborn. The first thing they teach you about parenting is that it's a surrender of control. Okay: the first thing they teach you is to take that diaper immediately out of your house and bury it in a nine-foot hole as fast as possible. But the second thing they teach you is about the surrender of control. And this gives parenting a kind of breathless feeling, frightening and exhilarating, especially if you are someone who thrives on schedule, arrangement, and punctuality. A child does not adhere to any kind of preexisting arrangement. Abandoning this expectation can be the greatest liberation of your life.

Like nothing else, parenthood makes you realize, sharply, that you are now in the position of the advice giver. You are the role model, the example, whether you are ready or worthy or not. It goes without saying that the best example is the example quietly set, but this is not always convenient, or realistic, as we are all prone to lapses and embarrassing behavior and tantrums of our own, especially between 4:00 and 6:30 P.M. on the expressway—*don't tell me that eighteen-wheeler full of chickens has run out of gas*. We are not always our best selves. And yet here we are, at the wheel, assigned with the task of shaping a real-life human or humans. And with the slightly nauseating rush of that assignment comes an appreciation for all the advice you've ever received before, especially from your own parents. Like you, they weren't perfect. But they probably did the best they could.

I didn't know it at the time—none of us did—but a few months after this visit, my father would become very sick. Our lives would change; all our energy was dedicated to improving whatever time he had left. A high school science teacher, my father was full of wonderment about how the world worked—he was the kind of person who could spend an hour explaining the Northern Lights, or the inner workings of a toaster oven. Suddenly his world shrank. For the coming year, life would not be about the big play, the grand gesture, or long-term plans. The focus would be on creating smaller, perfect moments that brought us all temporary relief and happiness.

Little victories.

The advice in this book is both practical and ridiculous. It is neither perfect nor universal. A few years back I began writing advice "Rules" columns for the *Wall Street Journal*—Rules of Thanksgiving Family Touch Football, Rules of the Gym, Rules of the Office Holiday Party. The idea was to make a little fun of the Cult of Advice, the absurd surety of know-it-all experts and, of course, our blossoming era of inane Internet lists (29 WAYS TO WATCH A SUNSET WITH YOUR PONY!). Ours is a culture that is always telling people what to do, but what do we really know? We're all still learning. Everyone's flawed. Everybody drops their ice cream on the floor, hopes nobody saw it, picks it up, and eats it. Please tell me that's not just me.

You can read this book in order or out of order. You can read it on the train, the plane, the beach, or in the bathroom. Go ahead, I don't care if you put it in the bathroom. Put it right next to the can, atop that 1991 copy of the *Sporting News* and that giant book about architecture that no one's ever opened.

The assembled madness here is the product of many life mistakes, made worthwhile by a handful of those little victories.

★ When I first dreamed about writing a book, this was not the book I dreamed of writing. I imagined a distinguished novel, thick as a curbstone, sold in stores where the clerks were wild-haired and prickly and didn't need a keyboard to tell you that the Pynchon was around the corner, sharp left, behind the vegan cookbooks and the guy pretending to read Sartre but really reading that book about waterskiing kittens who solve mysteries. My book would be the kind of book that would be hard for me to write and hard for you to read. It would be well reviewed to the point that authors I didn't know became envious and authors I did know became inconsolable. I would read my book aloud at colleges and public radio stations, and if I could smoke a pipe, I would smoke a pipe. I would probably wear a vest. A tweed vest. There would be book parties with terrible wine and someone at the end would force you to buy a copy. I would sign your copy. My signature would be unrecognizable. You would wonder if that was a signature or if an insect had been crushed between the pages. The book I dreamed of writing would not make me rich, but it would make me soulful, beloved, cultishly popular. I would not be famous (*eww*) but respectfully known (far preferable). I would give intense, rambling interviews to impressionable students in which I would speak about "craft" and my isolated writing jags at my cabin in Vermont, even though I do not own a cabin in Vermont. Once in a while I would be recognized on a subway or at a food cooperative and I would blush, because I did it: I wrote the book I dreamed I would write.

★ This is my way of explaining I didn't wind up ghostwriting Jessica Simpson's autobiography.

★ This is not Jessica Simpson's autobiography. I am sorry. This is a rule book. There have been rule books before— stacks upon stacks of them—but this book is unlike any other rule book you have ever read. It will not make you rich in twenty-four hours, or even seventy-two hours. It will not cause you to lose eighty pounds in a week. This book has no abdominal exercises. I have been doing abdominal exercises for most of my adult life, and my abdomen looks like it's always looked. It looks like flan. Syrupy flan. So we can just limit those expectations. This book does not offer a crash diet or a plan for maximizing your best self. I don't know a thing about your best self. It may be embarrassing. Your best self might be sprinkling peanut M&M's onto rest-stop pizza as we speak. This book is not a four-hour career plan or a four-hour workout or four-hour anything. I appreciate a good hustle, but there are only two things in life that take four hours: the drive between Philadelphia and Syracuse, and baking and eating two entire trays of brownies by yourself.

★ I cannot promise that this book is a road map to success. I would, however, like for it to make you laugh. Maybe think. I hope this book can become your pal. You know those scenes in movies in which the protagonist has a chance encounter—usually on a train, or in a Greyhound station at 3:20 A.M.—with a stranger who offers unsolicited wisdom about the world? The stranger is kindly. He has wild eyebrows, and wears a hat with a hole in it. The stranger has lived things. Lost things. The stranger knows that love really matters. The stranger also knows that you should never serve soup at a dinner party. This book is that stranger. This book has wisdom both weighty and banal, and you don't have to wait in a Greyhound station at 3:20 A.M.

★ If by chance you are in a Greyhound station at 3:20 A.M., the bus to Pensacola leaves in three minutes.

★ Again, seriously: don't serve soup at a dinner party. Not as an entrée, at least. No matter how good it is, soup is always, you know, soup. You serve dinner soup to your family when two of you have the mumps. Serving soup as an entrée to guests is like showing up to collect an Oscar in flip-flops and a bathrobe.

★ Some of the advice in this book is big advice. Some of the advice is very detailed, specific to the point of making you uncomfortable. It favors the practical. I don't think we get anywhere with whimsical advice, the kind of airy nonsense that people say at graduation speeches. *Take a year off to learn the tambourine. Live in a treehouse! Fly a kite with a talking dolphin!* Great. Maybe the tambourine and the kite-flying talking dolphin can help you pay back $120,000 in student loans.

★ I prefer specific advice. I have long been obsessed with reading my horoscope, and everyone knows that there are two types of horoscopes. The first kind is your classic, imprecise, crowd-pleasing horoscope designed to appeal to as many people as possible. *A kind act today will change your outlook. A rich soul measures fortune in friendship.* Those are useless and horrible. You can use those horoscopes for the hamster cage.

The other kind of horoscope is specific and spooky in detail. It does not mess around with vagaries. It says stuff like *Tomorrow do not wear green socks.* Or, *In the afternoon you will be visited by a middle-aged man with a falcon on his shoulder, who will try to sell you a broken Camaro.* This is unnerving advice. Specificity is intimacy, of course. The best kind of horoscope makes you look over your shoulder. This is the kind of advice I wish to offer you.

★ Tomorrow do not wear green socks.

★ In my day job, I spend a lot of time following professional sports, and if you follow professional sports, you learn a few things that might not be apparent on TV. The first thing you learn is that professional sports are professional. I know that sounds dumb and obvious, but it's the cleanest way to put it. It's a *job*. If you're a pro athlete, you're not supposed to describe your job as a job, because you are doing something that most people would do for free, unless, of course, they were good enough to do it for $15 million, in which case they would never do it for free. And yet you can still tell the difference between the athletes who still love it and the athletes who wish they could get away from it. One of the quiet agonies of life is seeing people who loved something lose touch with what made them happy. It can happen to anybody, not just members of the New York Knicks. No matter what you do for a living, where you live, or who you're with, it's important to remember why you wanted to do something for the first time. How it made you feel. Why it made you happy. I think that's an emotion to reach back for, always.

★ Still, we should probably set aside the goal of total happiness. There's no such thing. Total happiness is just a bunch of it. All happiness is temporary. There's no permanent bliss. Even a genial Zen master in line at the supermarket can't believe the guy with $90 worth of groceries is walking back to Aisle 9 to get some KitKat bars. The genial Zen master is ready to smash a jar of mayonnaise on the floor. *How long does it take to find KitKats? You have to be kidding me.* Life is a comedy of minor furies. Everybody hates the airport, the dentist, the dentist's office, the magazines in the dentist's office, sixth grade, at least 40 percent of circus clowns, ten-minute parking, microwave bacon, and the alternative driving route through Connecticut. There is no strategy that is going to make you like these things.

★ But you really should listen to more Stevie Wonder. I'm not kidding about this one bit. Not the later, cringier stuff but the creative sweet spot between 1968 and 1976. Listening to more Stevie Wonder from this period will make your life between 5 and 10 percent better right there. I guarantee it. It's that good.

★ Also, spend a little more money on flowers. Just generally.

★ This book is not going to tell you to eat more kale. I believe we have all gotten the message on kale. This book is not going to tell you to call your parents more often, though you probably should call your parents more often—or, alternately, you should take away your parents' phones and hide them in the garage, which also does the trick. This book is not going to tell you to buy a hiking stick or reimmerse yourself in the great literary classics because . . . let's be real. You decided long ago to get through life without ever finishing *The Scarlet Letter.*

★ But I am not going to lie to you. I am going to be brutally honest. There are no lies in this book, except for the time I kissed Charlize Theron.

★ I humbly suggest that there is a way to maximize life, to get the most out of it, to develop a sense of adventure and chart a new path. Jeez—I sound like a TV commercial for a bank. Let me try that again: I believe it is possible to find, at any age, a new appreciation for what you have—and what you don't have—as well as for the people closest to you. There's a way to experience life that does not involve a phone, a tablet, a television screen. There's also a way to experience life that does not involve eating seafood at the airport, because you should really never eat seafood at the airport. There is a life inside you that you may never have known existed. This is the part where I am supposed to tell you to have a wild adventure, like trekking to the South Pole. I am not going to tell you to trek to the South Pole. Trekking to the South Pole sounds expensive and stressful. Plus it's freezing. Plus, there's not a Dunkin' Donuts for miles. Actually, I don't want to discourage you from trekking to the South Pole: Seriously, if you're heading out the door with skis and an ice pick, don't let me stop you. Hit the North Pole while you're at it—I think the North Pole has a Dunkin' Donuts.

★ Like the title says, I want us all to achieve little victories. I believe that happiness is derived less from a significant single accomplishment than it is from a series of successful daily maneuvers. I want to get you from the house to the car to Starbucks to the office and that useless 10:30 A.M. staff meeting to that ridiculous spinning class with the nonstop Katy Perry and then home again feeling as if you conquered the day. It's going to require some faith on your part. You're going to have to take at least 2 percent of this book seriously. You're going to have to accept some tough love. You're going to have to stop doing some things.

You're going to have to stop buying discount toilet paper. What is wrong with you? Discount toilet paper?

★ But little victories are real. At the moment, Jesse, the two-year-old, is snoozing on the couch near where I am typing. There was a period when my wife and I thought we'd never have a child. Setbacks nearly cut us in two. When my wife finally got pregnant, we spent the first half of the pregnancy waiting for the baby to vanish. It was not fun. And now I look over and he is sleeping and there's a little smile, like he's watching an episode of *Cheers* in his dreams. It feels like a victory. A little victory.

★ Of course, it's also entirely possible that before he fell asleep, Jesse stole my iPhone and dropped it in the toilet.

★ I believe we can all achieve little victories. Maybe it's the way you feel when you walk out the door after drinking six cups of coffee, or surviving a family vacation, or playing the rowdy family Thanksgiving touch football game, or just learning to embrace that music at the gym. Accomplishments do not have to be large to be meaningful. I think little victories are the most important ones in life. I really do.

★ Not kidding about Stevie Wonder or the discount toilet paper.

Hoard Your Friends

High school. Freshman year. An invite to a party, along with my best friend, Philip. Okay, it's probably not a party; it's more like a sad conclave of bored freshmen in ill-fitting clothes, maybe a half dozen of us, all boys, most of whom do okay in science class and can recite *Ghostbusters* line for line. There is a long and circular discussion of how the desired alcohol will be procured—elaborate, detailed brainstorming and planning from the brains of fourteen-year-olds who have little money and no car and need to be home by 10:30 P.M. We sound like we are planning a heist from the Louvre. All we want is a twelve-pack.

Suddenly Someone with an Unexpected Connect arrives with a twelve-pack of Milwaukee's Best. The Beast, we called it. Or, the Worst. We ask no questions and begin consumption on an upstairs couch.

You probably remember your first sip of beer—the sultry crispness of the yeast, the hints of harvest pumpkin, and the faintest whisper of elderflower. Okay, it did not taste like that. A fourteen-year-old does not think beer is yummy. And the Beast is the Beast for a reason. It is the cheapest of beers; it costs less than bird food and tastes only marginally better.

I think I had two. Max. Maybe two and a half. Philip is bigger, so he probably had three or four. I remember sitting there on the couch and waiting for some wild feeling to wash over me—a blast of adulthood in twenty-four ounces, a sudden urge to sing country music at the top of my lungs—but before anything happened, I noticed my watch.

Almost 10:30. Shit.

Philip and I fast-walked back home in the darkness. By now we were feeling it. Our steps got heavier, words slower, stupider things funnier, but I didn't feel completely aware. When we got to Philip's driveway, I said farewell and scurried off into the night, running down the hill to my family's house and slithering through the back door by 10:29. Phew.

Upstairs, my parents had already gone to bed. From the kitchen I called Philip at home. There were several long rings before he finally picked up.

"Philip?"

"Yeh."

"Is Jassin. How u pheeling from the beer?"

"Nossure," Philip said. "I sink I pheel it . . ."

"Defitly a buzzzzzzz."

"Buzzzz. Yeh, defitly a buzz."

"But is this wasssted?"

"I don't fink I'm wasssted . . ."

The next morning Philip's mother walked downstairs to her kitchen and saw the red light on her answering machine flashing. If you are under the age of forty, an answering machine was a highly sophisticated robot that answered the telephone, folded laundry, and lit cigarettes for families in the 1980s.

Philip's mother pressed the flashing red button.

"Philip?"

"Yeh."

"Is Jassin. How u pheeling from the beer?"

The machine had recorded the whole slurry conversation. It was the ninth-grade Nixon tapes.

Thankfully Philip's mom, Rosalie, was the rarest of all maternal species: the "cool mom." She had a reasonable attitude about teenagers and alcohol and did not immediately put Philip's head on a stick. To this day I remain grateful that she did not call my parents, who undoubtedly would have put my head on a stick and paraded it down our street. She did give us a light cautionary talk about responsibility, and drinking, and why it was probably not the greatest idea for us to be huddling up in a classmate's room and guzzling Milwaukee's Beast and then wandering home in the darkness. But deep down I think she thought the whole thing was pretty funny.

And we did get the message, and learned something important. Philip and I never, ever . . . drunkenly talked into his mother's answering machine ever again.

It is nearly thirty years later and Philip and I are still friends. Between us there are now four children, three college degrees (two of those are his), at least a dozen crappy cars (even split), and now an entire United States. Years back Philip moved to California, and that was that. He's never returned. I always secretly hoped he'd find his way back here, to the concrete grind of the East Coast, but he's a wilderness person, and if he doesn't see an owl every ninety minutes, he goes into anaphylactic shock.

We don't talk all the time. Weeks pass. Months, often. You find yourself doing that when you get older, letting friendships slide. It's both regrettable and unavoidable. Distance makes it hard. You cannot call your friend on the other side of the country—with two kids—and ask him if he wants to go drink a six-pack in the woods. Maybe you should. Maybe you need to call your friend on the other side of the country—with two kids—and ask him if he wants to go drink a six-pack in the woods. Maybe you meet halfway. In the woods of Nebraska. (I am not sure there are woods in Nebraska.)

As you get older, friendship becomes a maintenance thing. You don't change the oil as much. You run the tires down. You turn to it when you need it. (You pray the friendship is a Volvo.) And then moments happen that remind you why it's so important.

I had been living in New York City all of eight months when I got diagnosed with testicular cancer. I lived in a tiny apartment I paid way too much for, and I was mostly by myself and whacked out from the surgery and the radiation, and I couldn't really eat anything because I was pretty quickly puking it up. It was miserable, and I made it more miserable by shutting down to the outside, to my parents and friends, telling everyone I was more okay than I was, self-martyring, the whole bit.

The one person I'd been talking to through the whole episode was Philip, whom I still called Philip, even though he'd become Phil somewhere around seventeen and the only people left who called him Philip were me, his mother, and bank tellers. He was already out in California by this time, and over the phone he said the kinds of things that people say to people who are sick, about keeping your head up and pushing through. One night he called and asked how I was doing and if I was still puking and unable to eat. I have no idea what I said in response. Then Philip asked if my apartment was number 2 or 3. Before I could figure out what he was talking about, the buzzer to the apartment was ringing and there he was, all six-foot-five of him, freshly arrived from the airport on an impulse ticket that must have cost far more than his starting-out salary could support.

I didn't know what to say.

These days I see Philip in person a couple times a year. Maybe there's a lucky third or fourth time, when his business takes him back east or I find my way to San Francisco. It is why I cheer for the San Francisco Giants to make the playoffs, even though Philip could not name a Giant if you dangled him by his hiking boots off the Transamerica Pyramid. This friendship is one of the great joys of my life, and yet it doesn't feel like an accomplishment. It has survived distance and my flakiness and the natural atrophy of time.

And it is always there, still vital, essential, ready to be picked up where it was left off. Friendship like that is a treasure. I am buying a six-pack and I am going to look into the woods of Nebraska.

. . .

★ Friendship is good for you; we all know this. There are a zillion studies establishing that the more friends you have and the more socializing you do, the more satisfied and happier you are, the more money you make, the better sex you have, the more Grammys you win. More friends does mean that you will also spend a third of your salary on birthday presents and go to a lot of birthday dinners at loud restaurants where no one can hear anything, but I have come to believe this is a fair trade-off. As Philip knows, I am a friend who needs improvement. I too easily fall in and out of touch; I fail to return e-mails promptly; I am not interested in helping you move next weekend because, well . . . I have to go to my cat's art show. This is a personal shortcoming. This is an area I vow to improve. As I get older, the two things I want to work on are improving friendship and making a margarita without having to Google "How to make a margarita." If I can do those two things, I will be set. Nobody lies on a deathbed and wishes he had fewer friends.

★ I can't believe I typed that last bit. Terrible.

★ Can we just address the horrifying "nobody lies on a deathbed" cliché for a moment? It's the most hackish of all contemporary advice clichés, but it had to start somewhere. Who was the first person to exclaim "Nobody lies on a deathbed and . . ."? Was it actually from a deathbed? Who makes this bed? Was there always a bed? Everyone knows that beds were only brought to Earth in the early 1990s. Was it first a "death floor of reeds"? *Nobody lies on their death floor of reeds and regrets having a second mammoth burger—especially you, Ruk-Tu, who lived to a ripe age of nineteen.* Is there any table of evidence to support this life philosophy? The "nobody lies on a deathbed" genre is so stuffed with conventional wisdom. What if it's all butt wrong? What if people lie on their deathbeds and say, *You know what, I really should have spent MORE Saturdays at the office! I could have called my mom less. I hated that once-in-a-lifetime family cruise to the Antarctic. Why did I eat all those salads?*

★ On the topic of friendship, I take great inspiration from my wife, Bessie, who is the greatest friend I've ever seen. She is the person who does not just remember your birthday but attends it, with a gift that was not purchased on the way out of the airport but actually considered and wrapped, with a card, handwritten. She is interested in your high school reunion and your ultrasound and your mean boss at work, and will listen, raptly, to it all. She will like your milkshake-covered child on Facebook within minutes of your posting your milkshake-covered child on

Facebook. This quality has made my wife a very popular person, to the point where her friendships are like a second job and second life, with voluminous responsibilities, including what seems to be at least an hour on the phone at night. This might sound like I am mocking her, but I am not. It makes me admire her and love her very much and realize that I still have growing up to do and I am basically a weasel who buys gifts on the way out of the airport all the time.

★ The best type of friend is a no-brainer: the Listener. That's the kind of friend my wife is. There is always a place for the Listener. It's like knowing how to make children's balloon sculptures or deep-dish pizza. In life, there will forever be a place for you.

★ Hang tight to your friends from growing up. I know that is not always an easy task. Perhaps you moved often as a child and live in a completely different part of the world; perhaps you are very famous and your childhood friends are always hassling you for autographs and private jet rides; perhaps your childhood friends were imaginary and now have jobs working overseas. Understood. But it's helpful to have at least one person who remembers you before you became the person you are now. As you age, it's easy to forget or romanticize or even block out where you came from, and a childhood friend is useful for being that compass and reminding you that yes, you wore the same pair of red corduroys every day of fourth grade, and tried to grow a ponytail freshman year of college.

★ Yes, I had a ponytail freshman year of college. I didn't look anything like a hippie. I looked like a sixty-one-year-old guy who lost an audition to be Neil Diamond's keyboard player.

★ I would like to make the case for old-fashioned phone communication. As in actual talking, with your mouth. Like you, I live in a thoroughly modern world in which texts and e-mails have almost completely replaced verbal interaction: if I look down at my phone and notice that I am actually about to receive a phone call, I am fairly certain that the person on the other end is going to tell me an asteroid the size of Greenland is thirty minutes from barreling into Earth, and *I still debate letting it go to voicemail.* But I think *talking* to your friends is good for you. I think there's something emotionally satisfying about the experience. It is also nice to be reminded that not every phone call is a nightmare to be avoided. The person on the other end is not asking you if you would care to do a brief phone survey about your recent stay at the Courtyard by Marriott. The person on the other end knows you vomited in the passenger seat of Gil Hundley's parents' car.

★ Not long ago I was back home and I found myself driving past Gil Hundley's childhood home and wondering if, for some sort of cosmic justice, I should let Gil Hundley's parents vomit in the passenger seat.

★ Everyone these days has friendships that have gone exclusively electronic. I am on daily—sometimes hourly— e-mail chains with people I went to college with whom I have not seen in years. I can't decide if this is a terrific accomplishment or undeniably sad. We *are* in touch, after all. When my wife asks if I have heard from my old friend John V., I hear from John V. six times a day. I have seen photos of his kids, I know about his new job, I know his opinion about the New Orleans Saints defense, because he wrote three hundred words about it in a group e-mail this afternoon. But I have not *spoken* to him in five years. There is at least one guy on that chain who hasn't contributed since 2008. I am only 10 percent sure he is alive.

★ Apparently it took many, many weeks for Gil Hundley's parents to get the smell out. I heard about it forever.

★ My wife is a great fan of mixing friends, which is a dark art. She will mix childhood friends with work friends with college friends with someone she met eleven minutes ago on the sidewalk holding a boa constrictor. I respect her compulsion. If it works, it's a seamless and rewarding arrangement of lovely people who share a common thread: you. But this is tricky business. In my experience, the newer friends tend to integrate well, but the college and childhood friends quickly grow resentful and suddenly remember they have to head home and write a passive-aggressive text to you about your "fancy new friends."

★ This is going to make me sound like a crank, but I believe the culture is currently suffering from birthday party creep. Your parents had it right: they celebrated Dad's fortieth and Mom's fiftieth (though everyone joked she was thirty-nine, hee-har), and of course everyone goes for Mom and Dad's seventy-fifth because, you know, death! If

Grammy makes it to one hundred, ya gotta show and see if Grammy can still blow out the candles. Those are inarguable standards. Must-appears. But lately there is a trend toward celebrating every adult birthday, as if we are still nine years old. On the face of it, this is okay: in a world in which we are losing connectivity with our friends, we should take advantage of every opportunity to gather, and if that means marinating in a restaurant chair for four hours for someone's thirty-sixth birthday, watching them drink eleven glasses of rosé and slowly unwrap presents, so be it. But soon you are back celebrating their thirty-seventh. And this is where it begins to feel like an obligation. My wife, with her many friends, attends roughly six thousand birthday parties a year, a level of dutiful constituent loyalty that should get her elected to the United States Senate.

★ Twenty-one, of course, is a ritual. But do not go to a thirty-first, forty-first, or fifty-first birthday party. You do not publicly celebrate your forty-first birthday unless you are a highway car dealership.

★ Reunions are tricky. On paper it seems harmless: you're traveling to a place from your past; you're meeting up with former colleagues; you have no idea how they look or what they have become; you have to dress up; there's the extra twenty pounds you now carry; there's the fact that it's happening in a gymnasium where the varsity baseball captain once held you to the floor and farted in your face; there's the existential collision between the person you once were and the person you are now today; there's alcohol . . . okay, on paper it sounds completely terrifying. I would rather go on one of those "working vacations" where they wake you up at 3:45 A.M. to milk the cows on a dairy farm than attend my high school reunion. I prefer to revisit high school on my own time, preferably from a moving car doing at least 70 mph.

★ If you choose to attend a reunion, it's important to always have an evacuation excuse, a reunion "out"—you have quintuplets back at the hotel who need to be in bed by 5:15 P.M., or you just noticed on the drive to the reunion that your childhood home was on fire and you need to get back and put it out.

★ Related: be wary of visits with your friends to Ye Olde Stomping Grounds. I have done this; it seems like it's going to be great—you're visiting an old college bar you loved twenty years ago; the memories are going to come flooding back; you're going to dance around to the Temptations like you're Kevin Kline in *The Big Chill.* Then it dawns on you that you are a bunch of forty-two-year-old dads in the corner drinking Coors Light and eyeballing students who could be your children, and the rest of the room is asking, *What is up with those dads over there?*

★ When you go to a bachelor/bachelorette party, it is never one of your close friends who winds up being the Crazy Person at the Bachelor/Bachelorette Party. The crazy person is always the last-minute guest, the person from the office nobody really knows, who winds up stealing a horse.

★ It's smart to make friends in the workplace. But it's also important to keep friends outside your profession, who don't really care about your boss, or the latest petty internecine rivalries, or how awful the bagels were in that meeting. We all have to monitor our propensity for talking shop. I work as a writer, and if I ever find myself in a room full of writers "talking shop," I locate the nearest window, climb out onto the fire escape, glide quietly down to the sidewalk, and run as fast as I can for forty-five minutes in any direction.

★ Every group of friends has "the Organizer." This is the person who once a year sends a plaintive e-mail about Vegas or Sedona or a trout-fishing trip to Montana and then proceeds to get increasingly agitated as nobody responds for three weeks. *Guys, I am just checking in about Montana. If we want to book the lodge . . .* But every once in a while the Organizer pulls it off, and it's a great trip. (For two days, until everyone turns on the Organizer in a fight about how much the stupid lodge costs.)

★ Think about friendship as a lifelong ambition. Everyone hates to be told to "make new friends"—it conjures up haunted thoughts of your mother laughing to herself as she drops you off at a month-long archery camp. Friendship does not have to be a conscious act. It does not have to be explicitly stated. Life is not Facebook. But if you can maintain friendships deep into adulthood, this will enrich your life in ways you cannot imagine, and it will give you emotional ballast for all the relentless everything that is to come. We are now a terribly busy and technologically dependent species, and in the rush to stay connected and present, we too often disconnect from very human and necessary feelings of interaction. Friendship humanizes. You will appreciate this later, on your death floor of reeds, drinking from a can of Milwaukee's Beast.

Nobody's Cool, Especially Me

True story: I am many thousands of feet in the air, flying in a private jet with one of the most famous entertainers on the planet. This is how it's supposed to be when you're flying in a jet with one of the most famous entertainers on the planet: It's supposed to be cool. It's supposed to be awesome. This flight is coming straight from the MTV Video Music Awards in Los Angeles, where the famous entertainer has won the big prize of the night. This is going to be a party. Things will happen on this plane that aren't supposed to happen on planes, because the plane is ours, and if it's ours, anything goes, right? The famous entertainer provides all necessary airplane carte blanche. I will take in every second of this moment at 30,000 feet and have a story I can tell for life, repeat it *ad nauseam* until all my friends roll their eyes at each other when I begin telling it. I will always be very coy about saying who this famous person is, out of some obnoxious sense of protection. I will never say exactly who it is, because it is much cooler not to say who it is.

Okay, it's Rihanna.

And this is what it's really like up here: it is not cool. Not in the slightest. Everybody, including Rihanna, is asleep, except for me. I am pretty sure we are 30,000 feet in the air, but I am not sure what we are above. Maybe Colorado. Maybe Idaho. Maybe the Pyrenees. The cabin smells like uneaten Chinese food and what I think is stale pot. More than two people are snoring. The plane is a Gulfstream IV. Or V. Or maybe a Gulfstream III. I am not even sure it's a Gulfstream. I don't know anything about private jets; I drive a family wagon that reeks of spilled milk and graham crackers. I am up here because I have been promised an interview with Rihanna, and I am freaking out, because this stupid interview has to happen before the plane lands for a scheduled refueling stop. Rihanna was supposed to talk before the plane went airborne, but then she changed her mind. Then she was supposed to talk as soon as the plane went airborne, and she changed her mind. She ate Chinese food instead, and I sat there watching Rihanna eat Chinese food and play around on her iPhone, and I was thinking about all the questions she was not answering while she was eating Chinese food and playing around on her iPhone. Then Rihanna went to sleep. Rihanna's assistant came back to where I was sitting in the plane—there are only eight or nine of us on the jet—and said that she will wake up Rihanna when we are an hour from landing, and we can do the interview then. That was two hours ago, and I am pretty sure I am beginning to feel the plane descend. I look over at Rihanna's assistant. She is also asleep.

In this moment I am the exact opposite of cool. I am sitting in the darkness and I can feel the anxiety vapors lifting off the top of my head. My phone says it is close to 4:00 A.M., which was roughly our arrival time for our scheduled refueling stop in Minot, North Dakota. I say "our scheduled refueling stop," but I really mean "their scheduled refueling stop," because as soon we land, they're dumping me on the tarmac, and Rihanna and her gang will fly off to London, and I will find a commercial flight to Minneapolis.

And so I am panicking. I fear failure and I have a job to do. And so I get up, my neck scrunched, and find Rihanna's assistant sleeping in her seat. She startles, and whispers that she will do what she can. A short while later she returns and says Rihanna will see me now. I am making this sound like I'm sitting at the end of a long hallway. Rihanna is barely 10 feet away, now sitting up in her bed, which is the only bed on the plane. I move forward, down the aisle, and prop myself on the bed. I have interviewed a few people on airplanes and I have learned that it is important to get physically close to them—an airplane generates a lot of noise, even when nobody else is talking, and I've heard horror stories, including one from a reporter who sat on a jet with Bill Clinton for an hour and emerged with a tape recorder full of unintelligible fuzz. So I am getting close, leaning forward, across the covers. Rihanna is lying back on pillows, expressionless. I look like I'm going to read her a story in bed. I look like I'm going to read Rihanna *Goodnight Moon*.

And then we do the very unnatural but necessary thing of having a private conversation with people sitting quite close to us, about Rihanna's life and her career, and I try to glean as much insight and revelation as you can press into thirty or so minutes of a descending fuselage. Rihanna is as charming as a person can be expected to be when she has been woken up at 4:00 A.M. on a transcontinental then transatlantic flight for an interview with a nervous stranger. She looks amazing, even if she appears several times to be falling back to sleep. Her handbag does smell a little like weed, but then I read later that some leather handbags actually smell like weed because of the way the leather is treated, so it might not have been weed, but I don't know. I sound like I am making excuses for Rihanna, who can do whatever she wants, what do I care? Then the flight attendant on the jet comes over and says the flight is about to land and I should return to my seat. I return to my seat. The plane lands.

And like that I am off the plane, still in the navy suit I wore to the MTV VMAs, my tie knotted. I must look like a lunatic when I walk into the airport terminal, where a bearded man in a hat offers to drive me to the commercial gate, and on the way he tells me a little bit about Minot, which is in the midst of an oil boom, full of transplant workers, which explains the rows upon rows of rented pickup trucks in the airport and all the guys in overalls in the ticketing area. He doesn't ask what

I'm doing in my dumb suit and I don't tell him. I guess there's a chance he'd think it was cool. Probably not.

And it strikes me, the ludicrousness of cool, how situational and contextual it is, how even the coolest moments are never as cool as they seem. Here I am, an active participant in the coolness industrial complex—this flight will be turned into a magazine cover story, some true weapons-grade cool shit— and I am sweaty and sleep-deprived in this wrinkly suit and I feel like a Martian, out of it, insecure, in need of a juice box and nap. Months from now I will be able to talk about this moment with some cool distance—nothing solidifies the cool like the passage of time—and yet cool will never be an accurate representation of the moment. Cool fled the scene. Clammy anxiety was always the feeling of the moment. And maybe there's something to be said for being honest here, and admitting that coolness is almost always a pose and seldom real. Let's discuss and liberate ourselves.

★ No activity on the planet besides talking about real estate wastes as much time and creates more turbulent feelings of personal insecurity than trying to be cool. It's true. Trying to be cool may be the thing that unites us as a species—wherever you are in the world, there is someone who believes he or she looks cool in those jeans and that T-shirt, the fading one with the name of a nonexistent pancake diner—and yet it is mostly a failed endeavor. Somewhere between 19 and 20 trillion hours are lost every year trying to be cool. And yet by and large, none of us are cool. I am definitely not cool.

★ And no, I am not saying this in a way to make myself look cool.

★ Know this: cool is overrated. Freeing yourself from the relentless pursuit of cool can be the single biggest thing you can do to create personal happiness in your life, besides installing a zip line in your backyard or deleting Twitter from your phone. Please do not try to be cool. This does not mean that by the end of this chapter I will be advising you to wear a fanny pack and fill it with dog biscuits and AAA batteries. I just want to limit your cool panic.

★ Because cool panic is an affliction. You can safely break your life into two parts: the pleasant, happy stuff you did before you started trying to be cool (nothing you did as a baby was cool, and yet you were generally beloved) and the nightmare wave of anxiety that has followed you ever since you discovered there was such a thing as cool.

★ Everyone's story of how they discovered cool is thoroughly uncool. I first became aware of cool—or what I thought was cool—with the arrival of the mid-1980s TV show *Miami Vice*. A moody drama about a pair of midlevel South Florida detectives who dressed like divorced art dealers, *Miami Vice* made a comical effort to try and be cool. Great attention was paid to its look, its music, its taste in automobiles and wardrobe. I was transfixed. Soon I was attempting to style my preteen self as *Miami Vice*'s antihero, Sonny Crockett. I wore pastels upon pastels, formless cream-colored blazers, loafers without socks. I stared hard at the mirror, trying to force my face to grow a five-o'clock shadow that resembled the actor Don Johnson's. An obsession grew. I cannot remember a single classroom discussion from junior high, but I can tell you from memory that Sonny Crockett drove a midnight-black 1972 Ferrari Daytona Spyder 365 GTS/4. And that bad guys blew it up. Whereupon Crockett began driving a 1986 Ferrari Testarossa, which is the kind of car you drive to take Sheena Easton to an Orange Julius.

★ My dueling style reference at the time was Prince, around the time Prince was dressing like an eighteenth-century French aristocrat. So you had this alarming sight of a young kid trying to mix knockoff Armani and very puffy shirts and boots. It's amazing my parents didn't haul me off to military school.

★ Do teenagers try to dress like celebrities anymore? I know that people like Taylor Swift and Miley Cyrus are considered "style influencers," but I am talking about people dressing *exactly* like them, as if it were Halloween. There is a moment in the movie *Fast Times at Ridgemont High* in which Phoebe Cates is pointing out the various school cliques in the cafeteria to Jennifer Jason Leigh and she mentions the girls who dress as Pat Benatar. She doesn't mean stylistically influenced by Pat Benatar—she means dressed *as* Pat Benatar. I was too young to be part of the Benatar wave, but I do have a vivid memory of a kid in my junior high school who dressed exactly like Michael Jackson—skinny trousers, sequined glove, and the red leather *Thriller* jacket, which I didn't even know was possible to buy. This all sounds crazy now, but I remember thinking he was incredibly cool. Better still, the rumor swirling around school—to this day I have no idea if it was true; this was junior high, so probably not—was that this Michael Jackson impersonator was dating a teacher. So there's that. This kid dressed every day like Michael Jackson and he may have won junior high.

★ The other significant cultural signifier at the time for me was a March 1986 cover of *Rolling Stone* with the headline "MEET BRUCE WILLIS." I was blown away by how cool Bruce Willis was. I feel like I should be revealing this under oath at a war crimes tribunal.

★ Bruce Willis wore an earring, as did Prince, and I spent an inordinate amount of time plotting how I too would have an earring. Piercing an ear through legitimate means was out of the question—no beauty parlor would do it without the permission of your parents, and I didn't have the stomach or the coconspirator to do the job at home—so I spent long hours in my room trying to construct a wearable earring that did not require piercing. One afternoon in my mother's jewelry box I located a hoop earring that was simply a clip-on—to me, this was like locating a Honus Wagner baseball card in the attic. I quickly styled it by adding my downstairs house key (I believe Janet Jackson was dangling keys from hoops at the time . . . why am I admitting to this?), and then wore it with a pastel jacket and an Oxford shirt buttoned all the way to the top without a tie. Parachute pants (look them up) may also have been involved. I believed I looked cool. I did not. I looked like a jazz saxophonist playing the Hilton.

★ All of this is here to show that coolness is not an easily imitated or buyable quality, though it is constantly presented and sold as such. Wear these sunglasses; lace these shoes; listen to this music; buy this shower gel; try this restaurant . . . It is an exhausting escalator of nonsense that drains wallets and delivers little personal satisfaction, like blackjack and graduate school.

★ And coolness always becomes a torrent: there is no end game. You will eventually find yourself at that cool restaurant and be chagrined to discover that it is no longer the coolest restaurant—there's a restaurant that's become cooler than this one. And you get to that cooler restaurant and you are saddened to learn that yes, the cool crowd has moved on to another, cooler place. And you go to that place . . . No, just kidding. I am going to go to Applebee's.

★ Even if you find yourself, purposefully or accidentally, in the region of absolute cool, the officially sanctioned stuff, you will often discover that, as the cool priestess Gertrude Stein once said, there is no there there. You will have stepped within the velvet rope, perhaps even the velvet rope within the velvet rope, and you will have discovered that the couches are sticky and uncomfortable and the drinks all cost $18 and taste like Hawaiian Punch left in the sun. You have taken your family to the vacation destination ranked as the number-one cool vacation off the beaten trail, only to learn that the beaten trail is lying on the pool chair next to you, talking loudly into a cell phone. There is no misery quite like a gathering of people who believe they are the special ones, doing the coolest things imaginable.

★ This explains the Hamptons and much of Los Angeles.

★ There is this assumption among the cool-obsessed that aloof is the same thing as cool, which is why most places designated as "cool" are rude, socially inept hellholes. Actually acknowledging cool is considered deeply uncool, so if you happen upon cool, it is best to keep this observation to yourself. See, I told you this business of cool would make you want to hit yourself in the face with a meat tenderizer.

★ It is possible to unintentionally back your way into a modest level of cool. Time, distance, and obliviousness can do wonders to cool even the most uncool things. This is why old photographs of your parents come across as cool— you know, the ones where they are in leisure suits and giant sunglasses and smoking Parliaments poolside in Fort Lauderdale. Old photographs of your parents also come across as cool because you aren't in those photographs; you hadn't come along and ruined the cool. By the way, your parents also think these photographs are cool for this reason.

★ There's this assumption that parenthood makes people uncool, and this is true in degrees—Batmobile mechanics bearing blowtorches could not have made my Honda crossover look cool—but in a lot of cases the parents were deeply uncool before the kids came along. I certainly was. I was happily going to bed at 9:45 on Fridays long before I had kids. I was making microwave mac 'n' cheese for *myself.*

★ But far worse than parental uncool is parents who think they are cool, which is the type of craziness you see in which a mother or father dresses the kid like they're about to play a set at the Coachella music festival. You know, parents who claim, "My kid really loves Wilco"—that kind of thing. Look, if you love Wilco and play Wilco around your kid, the kid will respond positively to Wilco. If you listened to a sleeve of nickels rattling around a dryer, your kid would respond to that just as much. Then one day your child will discover the Wiggles, and you would pay $2,000 to listen to a sleeve of nickels rattling around a dryer.

★ Not long ago I spent a solid hour combing the Web looking for a "cool diaper bag," and there really are such things, which promise to make self-conscious men look like Steve McQueen as they wander the suburban countryside, pushing a stroller and praying that their infants do not have explosive diarrhea. This is a lie. There is no such thing as a cool diaper bag. Why? Because it is a bag full of diapers.

★ By the way, do not purchase anything that promises to make you resemble the late Steve McQueen. There is an entire economy built on the premise of Steve McQueen cool, products of all sorts: sunglasses, motorcycles, automobiles, shirts, jeans, boots. It is a wonder there is not a Steve McQueen salad spinner, for that proper sheen of McQueen cool as you build yourself a proper frisée salad. Were Steve McQueen able to summon himself from the great car chase in the sky, he would be mortified at the commercialization of his coolness and scoff at the promises. Here is the cool thing about Steve McQueen: Steve McQueen. The end.

★ You are cool on your wedding day. I want to assure you of that. It's a nice thing. The irony is that you feel nervous and jumpy and you are sweating as you never have sweated before, but there is such goodwill toward you in the moment that it throws a blanket of coolness over you . . . until you dance the Electric Slide. Cool abandoned. Sorry. Wow.

★ The only real coolness is an unconscious cool. Actively trying to be cool never works, but occasionally you are cool when you aren't even thinking about it. You were not cool when you were a junior in college and you delivered a lecture in the stairwell of a party about Miles Davis based on eleven minutes of lifetime listening to Miles Davis. You were not cool when you wore Chuck Taylors to the prom (sorry, all male prom attendees 1987–2007). Your vacation to Tulum was not cool; neither was that $90 haircut, or that dinner at the new place down the stairs and around the corner to the other set of stairs, where it was packed and loud and the nachos tasted like a shoe box. But you may be cool at the exact moment you do not think you are cool. You were cool when you stopped everything you were doing to help someone, when you listened instead of talking, when you met the person who would become your partner and you were so nervous you could barely string words together. You are cool when you talk to your mother on the phone. Please do not let your mother know this, because telling her is uncool, and she will never stop calling.

Health and Sickness

My nuts ached on Sunset Boulevard. That sounds like the first line of a Raymond Chandler potboiler—or perhaps Warren Beatty's autobiography—but this was happening to me. It was the summer of 2000. The Democratic National Convention was in Los Angeles, and I was covering it for the *New York Observer*. At the moment I was sitting in Mel's Drive-In on Sunset Boulevard eating a chicken club sandwich, and every so often my, uh, junk would begin aching like hell. There's no graceful way of explaining this, so I'll just say this: I couldn't differentiate whether it was one ball or two balls or, you know, the whole deal. It was an occasional and overarching junk hurt, as if someone had taken a steel-toed boot to my crotch and then slammed it in a garage door.

The first thing you do when you feel pain in that region is

to ignore it as long as possible. This is idiotic, of course, perhaps life-threatening. Then you begin doing inventory on all the possible causes. *Did someone kick me in the balls recently?* No. *Did someone punch me in the balls recently?* No. *Did someone take a 30 kg Russian kettlebell, climb to the top of a twelve-story building, and drop it on my nether parts?* I do not believe so. Trying to self-diagnose through the Internet was terrifying. I grimaced reading about "torsion of the testes," a condition in which your spermatic cord is twisted as if you've asked your balls for fresh pepper.

By the time I got back to New York, the pain was dull and constant. I went to the doctor and the doctor did the proper doctor thing. He said it was "probably no big deal," but just to be sure, he was going to send me to a urologist.

The urologist was matter-of-fact. It was indeed something of a deal. "Seminoma of the left testicle," he said bloodlessly. "I'd like to schedule you for a procedure by the end of the week."

The "procedure" meant that he was going to cut an incision in my groin, reach in, and remove my left testicle, as if he were pulling a piece of Halloween candy from a purse. My reaction to this was something between horrified and incredulous, as if I'd been told a basset hound had just been elected president of the United States. I will spare you the part about how I freaked out and called everyone I knew for a doctor recommendation, and how I got a second opinion and the second opinion was exactly the same as the first. I was a classic case: right age, right symptoms, left nut. I'd been lucky enough to detect it early; it had not advanced.

If I acted now, everything would be fine. *Highly curable*, I was told. On the order of 96 percent. Maybe even higher. Close to 100. The news was presented like a winning scratch ticket: if you're going to get a cancer, this is the cancer to get! But even that 2 to 4 percent sits you up in bed and winks at you like a gremlin. If you tell somebody he has between a 2 and a 4 percent chance that day of being struck by a bus, he might never want to cross the street.

But it cannot be delayed; it's something you need to do. The surgery was set. I soft-pedaled the diagnosis to the handful of people I told, talking about it as if I'd turned my ankle in a pickup basketball game. I told Leslie, my girlfriend at the time, that it wasn't important for her to come down from Boston (where she lived) to New York (Leslie came anyway, because she was a good person). My boss at the *Observer*, Peter Kaplan, called me on the phone, sounding, as he often did, like he was talking beneath an airplane that had just turned on its propellers.

"JASON!" Peter said. "I KNOW somebody who went through this. The EXACT SAME THING. You're a YOUNG guy. You're going to be fine. FINE. OKAY."

I was anxious about telling my parents. It's the kind of call parents dread. No matter what you say to alleviate the worry, no matter how many times you repeat "highly curable" and "full and fast recovery," they are your parents, your mom and dad. I pleaded that they didn't have to be there, that this wasn't a big deal, that I'd be up and at it very soon. And of course it didn't calm my parents down, because there's no way it can calm your parents down. In the time I was explaining myself,

I think I heard my father drop the phone and drive himself and my mother 215 miles to New York, which I now realize is exactly what I would have done.

In the wait for the surgery, I would loiter in the Barnes & Noble near my apartment and thumb through the only book I knew about testicular cancer: *It's Not About the Bike*, by Lance Armstrong. I also celebrated my birthday. Let me tell you something about having your birthday right after a cancer diagnosis: people *really* show up. It was perfect attendance, on time and everything. We went out for burritos and margaritas and ignored the only thing on everyone's mind.

Meanwhile, I banked sperm. I'm just going to assume you've never banked sperm, so allow me to describe what it is like. Imagine the most erotic dream you've ever had in your life—I mean the really hot stuff. Now imagine the opposite of that. Banking sperm is like having an erotic liaison with yourself at 9:30 A.M. in a barren hospital Dumpster. Somebody hands you a sterile cup and sends you to a little office that looks like the room you might be detained in if airport customs found hash in your shoe. There is one chair, which you are frightened to sit in. In the corner is a small combination TV/VCR which you would have been pretty psyched about if your parents had given it to you for Christmas in 1983. There are VHS tapes with gag titles: I'm not sure there was a movie called *Around the World in 80 Lays*, but that kind of thing. There is a basket filled with wrinkled magazines you should not touch with tongs. They had *Juggs*. A lot of *Juggs*.

And in this desultory environment you are expected to have a tender moment with yourself and produce a sample, which will be frozen in a refrigerator at a rate of $400 a year. You have to sign paperwork indicating your consent and whom you would allow to take the sample in the event of your death. It is not advisable to sign it over to your mother, not unless you want your surviving family to end up on an episode of *Maury*.

The morning of the surgery I went to my friend Ali's and walked crosstown with her to the hospital. These were my final moments with two balls, and I wanted them both to walk the town, feel connected to the concrete, like Jimmy Carter at his inauguration. It was that time between summer and fall when New York is glowing and perfect, the way it is in Kate Hudson movies you half watch before falling asleep on an airplane.

The operation took less than an hour. It was pronounced a success. They confirmed that I had a malignancy, news that produced in me a weird reaction: *Good! I mean, bad?* (If you go through the ordeal, you want to kind of have the ordeal, no?)

A few weeks later I began radiation treatment, which involved going to visit a cancer center in Manhattan's West Village—a giant, sleek building that looked like a car wash for the Millennium Falcon. There I'd sit up on a slab in a sterile room and they'd close a big steel door behind me and zap my lower body. In the moment it doesn't feel like anything. But shortly afterward your guts begin to roil.

And you fear you might puke. And you do puke.

I'd spend the afternoons at Ali's apartment, which was close to the cancer center, sleeping in her guest room, puking in her guest bathroom (sorry, Ali). I was warned about going back to work too quickly, so of course I went back to work too quickly. I lost a lot of weight and didn't fit in my clothes. The first time I went to interview a subject for a story—the interview was at a W Hotel on the East Side—I ran straight to the men's room as soon as I got there and barfed my guts out. I spent the interview terrified that I smelled like puke, and as soon as it was over I was back in the bathroom, barfing again.

I wish I could say the experience instantly transformed me. I wish I could say there was an epiphany or a euphoric moment in that stall at the W Hotel in which I vowed I was going to change everything about my life. Nothing like that happened. My friend Mary, who'd been through cancer, said that you know you are on the other side of it when the stupid crap you used to get mad about before you got sick gets you mad again. Inane, petty things, like somebody not refilling the coffee in the break room at the office. Sweating the small stuff may be super-unhealthy for healthy people, but to a sick person it feels like a release, a return to normalcy, the healthiest thing imaginable. I hated thinking about the Big Picture all the time. I wanted to curse idiots in traffic. I wanted to be completely annoyed when the supermarket was out of Honey Bunches of Oats.

I spent a long time worried that I'd get sick again. If I sat still for more than ten minutes, I'd feel these phantom aches down there and think it was back again, ruthlessly charging after me for the second testicle. To this day I want no part of a hospital. When my kids were born, I was a basket case; my wife wanted to throw me out of the room like a nightclub bouncer. Shortly after our daughter Josie arrived, she got a nasty cold that turned into a respiratory problem; we spent seven nights in the ICU and I practically had to commit myself to an asylum. Everything turned out fine, but I freak out if a doctor closes a door. I know what a closed door can mean.

But the more and more I am away from it, the more I forget it ever happened. I honestly do. I go weeks and sometimes months not ever thinking about it. I don't feel special, spared, a survivor—if anything, I feel strange about calling myself a survivor, because I had it easy. The odds were my friend. I'm not even in the ballpark of someone who suffered. I don't feel a part of the club. I just feel like myself.

It is all anyone could really ask.

. . .

When Dad got sick, it was serious right away. He'd been having problems eating for a while; we'd gone on a family vacation in the Bahamas over Christmas—my parents; my brother, Chris, and his daughter, Blue; Bessie, Jesse, and I—and at dinner he ordered the same thing every night (plain pasta with vegetables), which I just chalked up to some bizarre old-guy behavior, like the chunky black sneakers he wore that made him look like a chimneysweep. In February, Dad finally got to the doctor—dads do doctors on their own time; a severed hand might get them to wander into an ER after thirty-six hours—and at first the doctor thought it was a kind of acid reflux. He was given a fistful of pills and sent home. The pain worsened. My mother began sending cryptic texts about "big tests" and making sure to pray. (Such pleas were not unusual; my churchgoing mother prayed for the Patriots to beat the Jets.) In early March the hammer fell: pancreatic cancer.

You probably know that pancreatic cancer is not a terribly curable form of cancer. It's actually a terribly incurable form of cancer. It's one of those diagnoses you tell people and they suddenly hush, because the assumption is that the diagnosed might have weeks or months, not years. There are exceptions—survival stories, whispers of advanced techniques and trials. The exceptions provide a useful life raft, but the doctors don't try to hide it: hard days are ahead.

Dad wanted to fight. Of course he did. My dad had grown up without much and he'd gotten an engineering degree and become a teacher and a high school tennis coach and he'd always maintained a mildly ornery, combative streak—he didn't put up with crap, or take crap, and he could be formidable in an argument (sometimes on car trips I'd listen to my father argue with whatever cuckoo talk radio program he was listening to, as if the radio host were inside the car, taking notes). He'd raised his children in the gentle suburbs, but he thought of himself as a city kid who wasn't afraid of concrete or conflict, who didn't back down, ever.

He would not back down here. Everybody wants to fight, especially at the start. It's the normal human reaction when pushed into a corner. You are going to be an exception. You're going to turn the odds upside down. There were scans to be done, and Dad needed to be fitted for a chemotherapy port, and from the looks of it he had already lost a bunch of weight, but he was going to beat it. We gathered in Dad's hospital room in Cambridge, not far from where he'd grown up, and it felt like a locker room in the minutes before a prizefight. He talked confidently and we talked confidently around him. He was going to get on the other side of this thing.

In the car home, we told each other the truth.

We had no idea.

That's not true: we had an idea, but we found it helpful to suppress it in favor of something more forward and positive. My mother, who would be at his side for the duration, saw the harshness of his decline but remained a beacon of optimism. Updates were presented with unbridled hope. *Daddy got the port installed today. Daddy just had his second chemo. Daddy is really ready to fight.* My mother, a city kid herself, who grew up not far from Dad, was a warrior. Between the two of them, maybe Dad could get on the other side of this thing.

But he was getting worse. I'd make plans to visit and have a bag packed, and he'd call moments before I left and ask me not to come. Well, he'd tell me not to come. He claimed he was worried I'd bring germs up—I had a kid; my house was a germ factory, he said—but there was more to it. At night we'd put Dad on the iPhone FaceTime with Jesse, and you could see that he was vanishing. By mid-April he was down fifty pounds. By late May it was closer to seventy. In two months he had lost more than a third of himself.

I stopped asking for his permission to visit. I just showed up, marched into the kitchen and through the living room to find him in the den. His hair had been slow to fall out—he had that going for him—but he was shrinking down to his bones. In the kitchen my mother pulled me aside and asked me how he looked. *I see him every day*, she said. *I don't know.* I'd tell her something between what she wanted to hear and what she needed to hear. I said he looked bad but seemed to be hanging in okay. Then I'd call my brother and tell him I'd seen a ghost.

There were times when he'd talk a little and times when he didn't want to talk at all. He mostly sat in front of the TV and faded in and out. The Red Sox were in the midst of a terrible season, and he watched every Red Sox game. That's how sick he was. He'd never been a loyal viewer of a sitcom in his life, but he developed an affection for *The Big Bang Theory*. The geek in him liked the inside math and science jokes. Sometimes in the darkness he'd be watching *The Big Bang Theory* and he would let out a huge laugh that sounded more like a pained howl. At first those howls scared me, but I grew to love them. They reassured me that there was still something fierce inside.

His weight became a crisis. He was on a strong trial form

of chemotherapy designed to shrink his tumor and make him a candidate for radiation and surgery. But it was wrecking his ability to keep anything inside. He grew terrified to eat, fearful of vomiting and diarrhea. Chris ordered crates of high-calorie drinks sent to the house. They were the worst thing you ever tasted, kind of like cream of chalk chowder, but if Dad could keep them down . . .

He couldn't keep them down. Or he ignored them altogether. It drove my brother crazy, but mostly it made us all so sad.

In early June he went to visit the doctor for a checkup, and when they got a look at him, they rushed him straight to intensive care. The cancer center at Massachusetts General Hospital was a shiny cathedral of glass and steel. Dad had a room with a zillion-dollar view of Beacon Hill and the golden dome of the statehouse. He never looked.

My brother and I began to talk about days left.

At the hospital they decided to feed him intravenously, which helped. If nothing else, he wasn't losing weight. But chemo was ruled out for the time being. His body couldn't take any more of it, at least not at the moment. It was crushing him.

He had to gain weight, or he didn't stand a chance. My brother tried to rally everyone to be Dad's weight-gain team. Chris elegantly called it "Team Not Fucking Around." He bought this pancake mix that would help Dad make pancakes with as many calories as a whole lasagna. Dad swore he would drink the cream of chalk soup. We looked into buying him pot. (You *really* learn who the potheads in your life are when a loved one has cancer. People were *lining up* to give us the phone number for their pot guys.) No suggestion was off the table.

I was due at the World Cup for work in a couple of days. I didn't want to go. Chris, a soccer nut, thought I was crazy.

I thought Dad would die while I was gone.

I flew back to New York in the morning and turned around to Brazil in the afternoon. As the World Cup began, I felt this unsettling combination of excitement and total detachment. The games were these brilliant bursts of energy and life, but I was consumed by what was going on back home.

Then the strangest thing happened: Dad began mildly to bounce back. Halting chemotherapy threw the ravaging of his body into reverse. The intravenous nutrition stabilized him. He put on weight. Then there was the Ritalin the doctors prescribed to give him a boost, and did it give him a boost. Soon Dad was calling me in Brazil three times a day. Three times an hour. Early in the morning. Midafternoon. Middle of the night.

He'd said maybe a hundred words to me in the past two months. Suddenly he was a seventh grader on his way to a school dance.

What's going on?

How is Brazil?
Where are you now?
What are you doing?
What are you doing?
What are you doing?

You know that scene in *E.T.* when everyone thinks E.T. is a goner and Elliott says his goodbye and suddenly the alien springs to life and starts yapping nonstop? It was like that. Dad sounded like Dad again. In early July, Mom sent a photo text message: she'd taken Dad out to dinner at a restaurant by the water. A couple weeks before, Dad hadn't been able to go for a walk around the block. He didn't want to go in the yard, get in a car, even come downstairs sometimes. Now I was looking at a photo of him sitting at the bar—the bar!—of a restaurant, digging into shrimp cocktail.

It felt like a rally, like he was getting a chance. Not long after coming back from Brazil, I went to Boston for his doctor's appointment, and the mood was almost festive. Dad had gained close to 10 pounds. We gushed over his new enthusiasm, energy, his interest in the world around him. He was having better days.

The doctors warned that they'd done nothing to halt the cancer—they'd just stopped the treatments that had been ripping him apart. The bounce was real, but that's all it was: a bounce. Gravity would soon pull him back toward earth. He needed to think about chemo again. He needed to get back on a regimen. Grim things lurked around the corner.

But it was hard to see the life that had returned to Dad's

eyes and want to put him back in that hole again. The choice was left to him. After a brief consideration in the doctor's office, Dad said he was going to take the rest of the summer off. The mood was different than it had been a few months before, when it had felt like a prizefight. Dad was going to chill. He was going to see how it went. He was going to try and live a little.

It was all anyone could really ask.

Look at the Stress on Him!

By now we all know that stress is terrible—not just emotionally but physically. Stress corrodes us, withers us, crushes us, and if we're not careful, it could kill us—or at least lead to us rolling around on the floor of a family restaurant screaming that it's been twenty-five minutes since we ordered the honey-dipped wings—*no, it's been twenty-eight minutes since we ordered the honey-dipped wings!*

The doctors and your Wednesday yoga instructor will tell you that most stress is avoidable, that very little of it is worth getting worked up over, but that perspective is hard to summon when your flight is being called and you're stuck in line at the airport newsstand behind someone taking a half hour to buy breath mints and *The Economist*. Situations like that, people tend to exhale loudly, as if they're getting a physical in a doctor's office. You know that exhale. It's the you-have-to-be-kidding-me exhale. You think the person in front of you didn't hear you. They heard you all right.

Let me appeal to your vanity here. Stress can indeed damage your heart and send you to an early grave, or, worse, turn you into a Hollywood publicist, but stress should mainly be avoided because it is a horrible face to put on. Acting stressed out is among our least desirable human behaviors, right up there with clipping your nails on the train. Nobody ever talks up a potential date to a friend as "Great hair, nice teeth—and oh, by the way, *hugely stressed.*"

Look at the stress on him/her!

He/she was a great boss—totally stressed all the time!

All I want is some Barry White, a bathtub full of champagne, and, you know, a hot night of stress.

We can all do better. Every time I am locked on the turnpike or shoving myself into a subway car or venturing out to the supermarket at peak weekend supermarket hellscape time, I tell myself I am going to keep calm. I will not fall prey to petty anxieties about long lines or lack of parking or the customer at the cheese counter offering an eight-minute lecture on his preference of comté over Gouda. And yet I backslide. I freak out. I get nervous and sometimes shouty—though my shoutiness is less like Bobby Knight and more like Don Knotts trying to find a lost duck. Mostly I am frightened, and I want to eat an entire package of Halloween candy corn.

Deep breaths, we are all told. But sometimes it's hard to find those deep breaths.

It may be helpful here to categorize stress.

ACTUAL STRESS

Traumatic health event
Suffering of loved one
Workplace termination
Bear attack, hawk attack, bobcat attack
Middle seat on airplane

PERCEIVED STRESS

Heavy traffic
Public speaking
Job interview
Overflowing toilet
New York Knicks basketball

NOT STRESS

Boss hasn't returned e-mail
Putting
Netflix is buffering
They're out of French vanilla
Anything to do with fantasy football

OLD-FASHIONED STRESS RELIEVERS

ALCOHOL. *Upside:* Produces temporary feeling of merriment, alleviating anxiety. *Downside:* You may take off your shirt and dance on top of bar at the office Christmas party.

ILLICIT DRUGS. *Upside:* Produces temporary feeling of merriment, alleviating anxiety. *Downside:* You think you're taking off your shirt and dancing on top of bar at the office Christmas party, but it turns out to be a school bus.

EXERCISE: *Upside:* Produces full-body physical release, alleviating anxiety as well as helping you lose weight and get a whole new outlook on life. *Downside:* Nobody wants to talk to you anymore in the office.

NEW STRESS RELIEVERS

THROWING A 2-POUND BAG OF FLOUR AGAINST A WALL: There is no downside to throwing a 2-pound bag of flour against a wall—it feels totally fantastic.

ADULT TIME-OUT. Any parent is familiar with the common child-rearing strategy of a time-out, in which the offending child is sentenced to temporary banishment to a crib or a bedroom or the city sewer system. It's a fairly effective practice, or at least offers the impression of effectiveness; my favorite detail about time-outs is that most little kids forget what the time-out was for within ninety seconds of banishment (after that, they're just entrapped in a maddening Kafkaesque nightmare). But you know who time-outs can really work for? Adults. Think about it. Every time you get aggravated at work, your boss instructs you to leave your desk and go sit in the office time-out room, which is a room apart from your maddening coworkers and, you know, your job. Stress gone—instantly. You might wind up enjoying time-outs so much that you become antisocial and petulant just to get them, at which point you will be promoted to CEO.

SOUP. I know I said I didn't like it at a dinner party but I love it as a stress reliever. If you are feeling stressed out, eat some soup. It's impossible to be anxious eating soup. I've tried, many times. You just can't do it. It's just you and a bowl and a spoon and some soup. See, you're feeling less stressed already. Soup! It is magical.

There were times I was stressed out writing this book. I loved writing this book, but it had been a hell of a year with Dad's illness, and there was a stretch during which it became very difficult to compose myself to write or even think about the book. This torment was unusual for me; I write a column three and sometimes four times a week, and it brings me a great deal of joy. This period was not joy. If I had overheard someone saying, *Who would like to spend eight hours cleaning up a pig barn?* my arm would have shot into the air. I would have loved to have cleaned the pig barn. I would have cleaned *pig barns*.

After one afternoon of writing very little, I came back to my apartment, opened up the bathroom door, and, after staring in my mirror for a while, lay in the empty bathtub in all my clothes. It felt like the kind of dramatic thing that Cate Blanchett might do in a movie. I'm not saying that Cate Blanchett has lain in an empty bathtub in all her clothes in a movie; it just seems like the kind of thing she might do. The scene was ridiculous—I still had my hat and my shoes and my jacket on—but I was stunned at how comfortable it felt, how genuinely soothing it was to lie crunched up in the porcelain.

I mentioned this behavior to a friend who had written a book.

Sounds like you are writing a book!

Okay, maybe it was predictable behavior, but it frightened me a little. So I did the thing I do when I get like that.

I got on my bike.

Let me backtrack for a second. When I met my wife, she rode a bike all the time in New York City. I thought this was completely crazy. This was before New York went bike nuts, with bike lanes and bike rentals you can use to scoot all over town. Back then I thought riding a bike in New York was about as safe as being a heroin addict. I worried about Bessie constantly, and when she would call to say she was riding over the Brooklyn Bridge to visit, I would pace my apartment floor like the widow of a whaling captain. It just wasn't a good idea, biking in New York. It stressed me out. If we were going to be a couple, she needed to stop riding. I was going to give her an ultimatum. Me or the bike.

Yeah, so I got a bike.

My dad unearthed a mountain bike I'd had in my parents' garage since college and brought it to New York. My first rides around Brooklyn and Manhattan, I felt like a child with training wheels. I'd go a few blocks and that was that. I bought a helmet, lights, reflectors (yeah, reflectors). Bessie had joined a cycling club that put on spandex and went for long, sometimes hundred-mile rides outside the city. I thought this too was insane. There was no way I was going to ride a bike one hundred miles. And there was definitely no way I was going to wear spandex.

I wore spandex. And rode a hundred miles. Of course I did.

I got a little addicted to the bike. But it felt like a good addiction. I have tried many things over my life to quiet anxiety—talk therapy, medication, listening to Norah Jones, looking at slideshows of Northern California real estate—but nothing has worked like the bike. For me, a bike has a 100 percent anxiety-quell rate. It is an antistress machine.

In August of 2014, Robin Williams took his own life. I'd interviewed him once, maybe six years prior, and the point of the interview was to talk about a comedy special he had made, but when that conversation was over, I asked him about bikes. Robin Williams was fanatical about cycling. You know when you're talking to somebody at a party about their job and they give very autopilot answers, and then when you talk to them about something they really care about, like the drum kit in their basement or their home bourbon distillery, they suddenly turn into the very exuberant eleven-year-old who still lives inside? It was like that. Robin Williams began animatedly talking about bike riding and his bike collection (he had a bananas collection) and his trips to the Tour de France. He sounded like a different person. His happiness poured over the phone.

At the interview I asked Williams why he loved to ride his bike so much.

It's the closest you can get to flying.

That line hits me like a hammer whenever I am on the bike, because I know it to be true. I mentioned it in a column I wrote after Williams died, and was struck by how many people wrote back to me about how a bike had saved them in hard times. *That's exactly the way that I feel too,* they said.

After pulling myself out of the empty tub, I changed my clothes (the spandex!) and headed off on my bike. It worked, immediately. It always works. There is something about transitioning from sitting still to moving that activates something vital and important and flushes all that bad and unnecessary and foolish energy away. It *is* close to flying. Once I am on my bike and the trees and the city are rushing by, I start to forget what I was stressed out over. Consuming problems suddenly become very small. Perspective arrives. Stress is unavoidable but mostly a waste of time.

If not, there is always the soup.

A Brief but Hopefully Compelling

Case for Marriage

★ Marriage has a ghastly PR problem. Though the divorce
   rate has been declining, fewer people are getting married,
   and the people who are getting married are getting married later. If you go to somebody's house for a barbecue,
   it is only a matter of time before a guest has six beers and
   begins to inveigh loudly about how the institution of marriage is a sham, how it's a violation of nature's will, how
   monogamy is an outmoded expectation that might have
   made sense for power-consolidating families in AD 600
   but makes little sense now, when there's, you know, high
   school flames you can look up on Facebook. This well-
   versed marriage critic will then burp loudly and fall asleep

in a lawn chair for the rest of the night, which says all you need to know about his marriage.

★ I am wary of any married person who says that if he or she weren't married, his or her life would instantly become a bacchanalia of unattached reverie. I think a more honest answer is that it would instantly become a bacchanalia of ordering Thai food and lying on the couch and watching the E! channel.

★ I like being married. I do. I know that doesn't sound edgy or modern, but I am comfortable with my decision. I threw out the receipt a long time ago. I am realistic about who I am, and I know that if I weren't married, I would not be the kind of rakish bachelor who attracts a crowd of women in a Monte Carlo casino. I would be the kind of rakish bachelor who goes to the zoo by himself. On a weekday.

★ I wish I'd gotten married earlier, I really do. I didn't need those five extra years of microwave chicken tenders and watching *SportsCenter* in the morning.

★ It is very common among successfully married people to describe marriage as "work." Part of this is clearly true—a marriage requires effort and punctuality, and there tend to be a lot of meetings. But I always cringe at how married people say "work"—they say it like the work is busting rocks on a Russian plain, not renting surfboards in Imperial Beach. I don't want the work in my marriage to feel like prison license-plate manufacturing. I want it to feel like a chocolate chip cookie factory that is open only two hours a day.

★ This is not to say that marriage is always easy, or devoid of conflict. If you have been married for a few years and you have not spent a few nights on the couch, I am pretty comfortable concluding that you do not own a couch.

★ As a married person, you are presumed to be an expert in marriage, and you will occasionally find yourself in a situation of advising a friend who is in a relationship but not married as to whether he or she should get married. This is a strange responsibility, and the odd thing is that your answer can vary depending on the day or even the time of day. You should be candid with your friend about the challenges of marriage, but mainly you should get to the really important, core issue, which is to dissuade him or her from inviting 350 people to a destination wedding.

★ Know where you stand on brunch. You can endure through sickness and health. No marriage is strong enough to survive two people who disagree about brunch.

★ Brunch is actually the third leading cause of divorce in the country. You can go to any divorce court and you'll hear a lawyer get up and say, "Your honor, these two people love each other very much and treat each other with kindness, but the husband here likes to go to brunch for four hours on Sundays." To which the judge invariably says, "Good Lord" and grants divorce immediately.

★ Of course, no matter how you feel about brunch, once children come along, brunch is out of the question. I would rather fly across the country with a 1,200-pound marlin in my lap than sit with a child through an extended Sunday brunch.

★ You don't have to agree on favorite movies and favorite music to be a happily married couple. Also, nobody believes that both of you love *Caddyshack II*.

★ I think a good marriage should surprise you. Now of course there are big, bad surprises in a marriage, like walking down the street to a random part of town and discovering that when your spouse said he or she was off on a business trip to Charlotte, your spouse is actually . . . well, your spouse is at brunch. That's a crusher that no marriage can survive.

I mean the smaller, happy surprises. I am lucky to be married to a woman who surprises me every day. Bessie is the only person I know who has owned and operated a hamster-breeding business, joined a circus, ridden a bike across the country, had jobs caring for llamas, horses, and starfish, can speak pig Latin, drive a powerboat, fire a pistol, and fall asleep on the toilet, has worked in a jail with prisoners, emceed a bug-eating contest in college, and dressed up as Edward Scissorhands two separate times in one Halloween night (long story), and she speaks with great pride about the time she successfully peed into a water bottle while flying over Crater Lake in a two-passenger airplane. I feel I know all these stories, and yet very rarely does a day go by when I don't learn something new, like the times a teenaged Bessie would sneak out of her bedroom, jump off the roof in her pajamas, and change into clothes she had hidden in a bag in the backyard, or the time she got a job taking care of an armadillo with eczema. If someone you love can surprise you like that, it's like discovering a new person every day. If someone you love can surprise you like that, I'd say you are more than halfway to a successful marriage.

And yes, I confirmed the story about the armadillo with eczema; it turned out to be totally true. Poor little guy.

Music for Weddings and Babies

and the Rest of It

When I look back upon my life, I will be most proud of two things: 1) my children (I am reasonably sure of this; don't let me down, kids) and 2) that people actually danced at my wedding.

My wedding to Bessie was an exciting event in my life, an indelible moment to celebrate a meaningful union with people we loved—yeah, yeah, yeah, all that. Mostly what I cared about that humid August evening in upstate New York was whether or not people danced. If people had not danced, I'm not saying it would have jinxed the marriage . . . Okay, it would have jinxed the marriage.

Everybody has been to a wedding where the guests do not dance, or dance only for a few minutes before wandering off the floor, never to return, and it is a special kind of cruel awkwardness. There is the happy new couple's pleading, doleful efforts to get people onto the floor—*C'mon, everybody, who doesn't love Christina Aguilera?;* there are the sad admonishments of the wedding DJ—*How about a little more Christina Aguilera?;* and there is the wedding band, hired at not insignificant expense, which knows an alarming amount of Christina Aguilera. There are the moments when you look out upon the floor and there is no one on it except for a second cousin who has had too much white wine. Dancing at a wedding is a hard thing to screw up, but somehow it gets screwed up all the time.

I was not going to leave this to chance. I spent hours and hours developing a perfect, dance-guaranteeing playlist. I worried about the music more than any other part of the wedding. I did not pay attention to invitations or RSVPs. Had the table arrangements been human skulls or the caterer served only stale walnuts and hot cocoa, I would not have noticed. As Bessie's cousin, Sam, officiated at our ceremony, my brain warred over two competing thoughts. My wife-to-be indeed looked beautiful. And, *did the playlist have enough Michael Jackson in the second hour?*

This is not a trivial matter. You're going to go to a wedding soon, or have your own wedding, or have a breakup and a new wedding that you don't even know you're going to have, and you're going to need this advice:

★ Stating the obvious here, but wedding guests want to
   dance. Like, really shake it. Your Aunt Claire wants to eat

two entrées and three pieces of cake and she's determined she can burn it all off with an hour and thirty minutes of nonstop wild-Aunt-Claire dancing. Do not deny her this privilege. You can hire a string quartet or a bluegrass banjo, but unless those guys can play a rousing rendition of "Brick House," send them packing to their rental van by 6:00 P.M.

★ Yes, you're playing "Brick House." Your wedding is not a moment to be a music snob; it is not a monument to your dense collection of B-sides and obscurities. You have the rest of your life to impress everyone with your knowledge of Berlin art rock and the majesty of Camper Van Beethoven. Today is not that day.

★ Live wedding bands fall into three categories: good, bad, and so-bad-it's-good. A good wedding band has mastery of its instruments and the principles of crowd entertainment and knows James Brown and a little Donna Summer. A bad wedding band might know all that stuff but insists on playing some of its own compositions, which will clear out the dance floor faster than a fire alarm. A so-bad-it's-good wedding band plays a slow *and* a fast version of "Careless Whisper" by Wham!

★ Sometimes a so-bad-it's-good wedding band is the right choice. Especially if the lead singer can't actually sing but wears a lime-colored tux and loves, loves, loves Lionel Richie.

★ If you hire a wedding DJ, be careful in your selection. Make sure he (or she) is open to what you want. You hired him; he should listen to you. If he brushes off your requests and says, "I've got this," please know: he does not have this. He is hoping you will like the same old Katy Perry and Electric Slide and Eric Clapton singing "Wonderful Tonight" as much as every other couple does. If a DJ rolls his eyes when you say you need to hear some Kool & the Gang, pick someone else.

★ Everybody loves Kool & the Gang at a wedding. It's why Kool & the Gang was invented.

★ I know somebody who had the *actual* Kool & the Gang as the band at her wedding, which I didn't even think was legal. This is known among reasonable people as the Greatest Wedding of All Time.

★ Be careful about soliciting requests from your guests. It's tricky. People like to make requests, but if you're not careful, you're dancing to five Phil Collins songs in an hour and then Cousin Stu drags the whole thing to a halt with "A Horse with No Name."

★ I am not saying you need to rent a smoke machine for the dance floor at your wedding, but think about it: how many more times in your life are you going to have a socially acceptable opportunity to rent a smoke machine?

★ "Brick House." Aunt Claire is asking. Come on.

★ Here is my basic wedding music strategy: follow a time-line. Start with the older stuff for your older guests. This doesn't mean you have to play Shostakovich or Hoagy Carmichael, but play something recognizable to somebody who may have voted for Nixon. Motown works in this regard. So does "Twist and Shout." Little Stevie Wonder and adult Stevie Wonder. The Four Tops. Your older wedding guests can move around for twenty minutes and call it a night. That's all they want. Then, ever so softly, glide into the present. James Brown. Jackson 5. Bee Gees. Prince. Madonna. Wind your way up to the inevitable onslaught of Katy Perry, Beyoncé, and Taylor Swift—don't be a jerk, everyone wants to hear it. Throw in the occasional hit anthem. George Michael's "Freedom 90." "Rock Lobster" by the B-52s. "We Are Family" by Sister Sledge. You can play "Rapper's Delight" by the Sugarhill Gang, but be warned, you can drive halfway across Pennsylvania in the time it takes to play the full version of "Rapper's Delight."

★ By the end of the night, the dance floor is just your drunkest friend dancing by him- or herself to "I Will Survive." (Nobody actually dances with a partner during "I Will Survive"; it's just a series of solo, triumphant interpretive dances.)

★ As long as I can remember, music has been essential to me. Isn't it to everyone? I am fortunate to be old enough to have learned about Bob Dylan by finding my dad's vinyl edition of *Blood on the Tracks*. I also am lucky to be young enough to know how to get iTunes to work without having to ring a bell in an assisted living facility. I can recall, vividly, standing in my friend Philip's kitchen as his brother, Wilson (yes, Philip had a brother named Wilson; yes, they have heard all the Wilson Phillips jokes), ran down the stairs with a tape cassette cued to RUN-DMC's "Rock Box," which sounded like it came from outer space (and it still does, brilliantly). I remember walking into a stereo store on the second floor of the Garage mall in Harvard Square and watching a guy remove a compact disc from a plastic jewel case and ask me if I wanted to listen to "The Future." I am old enough to have recently left a crate of "The Future" out on my front stoop with a sign that says FREE.

★ I am suspicious of any music criticism that sounds like nostalgic geezery—*In my day bands actually played their instruments,* yadda yadda and so on—but something has definitely been lost with the demise of record stores. I know there are a few record stores left, some really great ones, but most of them have been swept away by the Internet and digital music and it's a serious loss. Record stores didn't simply sell music, they created an environment that drove the fascination and helped create taste. Walking into a really good record store felt like an audition—for *you.* The record store wasn't trying to build your loyalty as a customer; you were trying to convince the record store that you were worthy of its loyalty. I used to worry about what I would *wear* to shop at the record store. Generally I detest any kind of haughtiness that verges on intimidation, but the kind of haughtiness practiced by good record stores had a certain utility. I am pretty sure that without it I would not have owned any Elvis Costello when I was thirteen.

★ Everyone's a secret music snob, but I am also distrustful of a person who doesn't appreciate the particular genius of super-duper cheesy pop, like "The Safety Dance" by Men Without Hats. "Safety Dance" may not be "Yesterday," but it will live forever. Every time you hear it in the car, you will crank it and sing it at the top of your lungs. This is underappreciated brilliance. You can name a dozen songs by U2, but you've never seen a car of teenage girls driving down the boulevard cranking and screaming out a U2 song. Ever.

★ Everybody has embarrassing music on their phone. And listens to it much more than they claim to listen to it. Everybody.

★ I find it very hard to get mad about the "state" of pop music. I feel people have been mad about the state of pop music my entire life. This is not to say there are songs or trends I don't get, or like, or even have the capacity to listen to. But it is to say that at this point, pop music is not intended for *me*. The whole business of pop music, in fact, is meant to appeal to something that's the opposite of me—someone younger, fresher, more eager. This is how it works. When you were thirteen years old, you did not say to yourself, *Wow, I'd like to buy this record, but first I need to know what all the fortysomething dads think.*

★ No matter how much you know about music, somebody will always know more. This is okay. You don't need to know the B-side to every Metallica single; you don't need to know where Morrissey was born. There's always going to be somebody who's a bigger fan, who's more hardcore, who's more of a lunatic. Somebody who saw them when, before they were ruined. This is mostly nonsense and not worth obsessing over.

★ Davyhulme. Morrissey was born in Davyhulme, in Lancashire, United Kingdom.

★ A bunch of years ago I was assigned to write a story about the teen group the Jonas Brothers, and this was my first exposure to the innards of teen pop, save for a few interactions more than a decade prior with stalkerish New Kids on the Block fans. At the point I caught up with them, the Jonas Brothers were pretty much the biggest thing on the planet for girls under sixteen; they played reasonably likable pop-rock music that sounded pleasant on a Ferris wheel or an escalator at the mall. But there was an odd purgatory to their success—very few late-teenaged or adult music fans took them seriously. If you saw a person over twenty-one there, chances were they were grumpily chaperoning someone (except for moms. There were some really crazy Jonas Brothers mom fans). But around the band was this anxious whirl of urgency, because people who'd been in the teen pop business for a long time knew that the audience would eventually revolt against them, that this had happened to everyone from Frankie Valli to Shaun Cassidy to those New Kids, and it was destined to happen to the Jonas Brothers too, no matter how gamely they talked about their musical maturation or transitioning to an adult audience or freeing themselves from their prepubescent admirers. In the course of pop history it had been discovered that the period of time from break-through to rejection was approximately thirty-six months. Within three years the Jonas Brothers' rabid, loyal audience would turn on them completely. This was an absurd notion at the time—here they were, selling out Madison Square Garden—and yet sure enough, it happened. Almost thirty-six months on the dot. And it underlined the disposability of pop, that you can't take it too seriously because nearly all of it fades away.

★ If you've obsessed over music, you've surely obsessed over what music to play in the bedroom—you know, when it's an opportunity for the nighttime romances. ("The night-time romances" is one of those safely neutered terms that cheeky married couples use to describe sex. It also sounds like the next bestseller from Nicholas Sparks.) What you do in your own private business is your own private business, of course, and I do not have deeply strong opinions on the matter other than to say, No Al Green, no Sade. This is not a slight upon either Al Green, who is inarguably one of the great voices in recording history, or the extraordinary Sade, who is kind of the chill female Al Green. It's just that both have become such cliché bedroom standards that it's impossible to put them on in the bedroom without looking like you just stripped down to a G-string and affixed a single red rose to your happy parts. If you bring someone back to your apartment and put on Al Green or Sade, he or she is completely allowed to double up on the floor and laugh like a hyena. I'm not saying you have to be counterintuitive—you don't have to make love to whale songs, or *This American Life*—but just take it easy on Al and Sade. I am fairly sure Al and Sade would have my back on this.

★ When we're young and dramatic and have big breakups, we tell ourselves we will never be able to listen to specific artists or songs—*That's it for me and the Captain & Tennille, never again*—but by the time you are married with kids you've forgotten what all those supposedly hurtful songs and artists are. It is true that everyone over forty has some vague feelings about getting dumped when they hear anything by the still-beloved Tears for Fears.

★ I am mixed on the generation of singing shows—*American Idol, The Voice*, and so on. On one hand, they're celebrating actual talent—they're not another reality show about a blended family of meth-cooking snake kidnappers. Many of the contestants are truly gifted, and a handful have gone on to find actual, deserved fame. But I worry that they're selling one very static version of singing, which is the extreme, hammy, grandiose version. It's hilarious to think what these shows would do if, say, a twenty-two-year-old Joni Mitchell showed up on the set. *Nice, pretty voice, Joni—would you mind trying to sing a little more like you're being chased down an alley by a truck?*

★ Concerts kind of suck now, because of money. Growing up, rock concerts felt slightly edgy and dangerous, like there was a 70 percent chance you'd see someone in the arena bathroom combing his hair with a knife. Now concerts have been corporatized and sold out to the highest bidder. This is all of our faults, actually; because the business of selling music has cratered so badly, it's put enormous pressure on live shows to be a profit center. The people who sit closest to the front aren't the biggest fans; they're just people who could pay the most, or know somebody who could pay the most. I am saying this as if I went to a lot of cool concerts back in the day, but you should know the first concert I went to was Sting, which is about as edgy and dangerous as a cider festival.

★ Until kids come along, there are not a lot of reasons to pay attention to children's music, or children's musicians, and I am not so far removed from being childless that I don't remember my distaste for the genre and its practitioners. This hostility vanishes upon parenthood. By now I have become accustomed to the mild grades of difference between Kidz Bop and Radio Disney. I have become obsessive, to the point of groupiness, with the kiddie band called Karen K & the Jitterbugs, authors of the hits "(I Woke Up in a) Fire Truck" and "Pancakes for Dinner." (Please tell me you know the words to "Pancakes for Dinner.") It's easy to look down on children's musicians because it seems so easy, singing about trivial things for a rapt audience, but 1) these are not minor things; pancakes will grow to have a much bigger role in your life than your junior high school girlfriend, and 2) if you watch an audience of kids around the age of two, you know they are anything but *rapt*.

★ When your child arrives, the books tell you it's important to sing to him or her, especially at bedtime, and you have visions of these wonderful parental duets, like vintage-era Carly Simon and James Taylor, sending your child into a long, blissful sleep. But what if neither parent is a singer? And what if by "not a singer" I mean can't sing—like, imagine a person singing, and then imagine a person getting his or her big toe stuck in an escalator and yowling for help. This is what our children must endure. Neither Bessie nor I can sing. We do not sound like Carly Simon and James Taylor. We sound like a pair of cats stuck on a roof.

★ And yet this is okay. It is not dangerous. It's still *you*. It's your voice. And there is something very natural, almost chemical about the way your child reacts to your voice, how familiar and comforting it is, regardless of whether you can hold a perfect C or . . . sound like a cat stuck on a roof. Do not attempt any vocal pyrotechnics. Hold your lane. You are not Aretha Franklin or Otis Redding.

★ Every parent has his or her closers, the songs you use to seal the ZZZs at bedtime. In our house, "Michael, Row Your Boat Ashore" is a closer, the encore. That's our "Born to Run." We don't play a show without singing it at the end. We've occasionally brought it out for a *second* encore. I used to sing "Wheels on the Bus," but my wife is convinced that "Wheels on the Bus" is too energizing a song—that there's something about those wheels, and once they start going round and round, Jesse is up pogoing in the crib like he's had four espressos. I don't know what it is about "Wheels on the Bus." At 3:00 P.M. on a weekday, somebody needs to sing *me* "Wheels on the Bus."

★ I have sung in public once in my adult life. At my wedding. Yes, the same wedding where I obsessed over the playlist. It was during the reception, in lieu of a toast. I didn't want to give a toast. Instead I sang a song by the Lemonheads called "The Outdoor Type" because it reminded me of my relationship with Bessie. When Bessie and I first met, I was not exactly someone who spent a lot of time, well, outside. (Early in our relationship we went on a hike and ended up having a ginormous fight because it was getting dark and I was scared and I wanted to turn around before reaching the top of the climb. Bessie, who would sooner sleep in a bear cave than not reach the top of a climb, nearly broke up with me on the spot.) Here is an example of the "Outdoor Type" lyrics:

> *I can't go away with you on a rock climbing weekend.*
> *What if something's on TV, and it's never shown again?*

I did not sing it especially well or movingly, but I tried. I tried effectively enough to be persuasive, which was all that was really necessary. I didn't need to arm-tackle the song. I was not brilliant, or in tune, or even close to in tune, but the effort was there. People who were there still talk about it. Music said something words could not. My wife still watches a video of it when she needs a reminder of why she married me, which is fairly often.

And then we went to the floor and played "Brick House," hell yes. People danced until 4:00 A.M.

Only a Game (But Not Really)

An open letter to my children's future Little League team:

Congratulations, motivated, ambivalent, or perhaps conscripted young baseball participant! You (and hopefully not your impossible nightmare parents) are invited to join the planet's least selective, lowest-expectation and most emotionally balanced youth sports team:

The Zen Cubs.

You may be wondering how we picked you to join an outfit like this. We didn't! We simply took a bunch of names off the wall and threw together a roster. Whoever wasn't wanted, we wanted—and "wanted" might be a stretch! There were no trades, no draft maneuvers, no rigging the system so we could land an All-Star-caliber shortstop. We have absolutely no idea what we have. Could be good. Could make the Bad News Bears look like the 1927 Yankees! Who cares? The mystery is part of the fun.

Now a few important words on life with the Zen Cubs:

Goals: The Zen Cubs will have no team goals other than getting exercise and having occasional amusement and trying not to break the windows on Coach's car, although we can all agree that the latter will be briefly hilarious. If you have a specific goal for the season— hitting for the cycle, throwing an inning of shutout relief, or proving to your parents that you really hate playing sports and would prefer to go to canoe camp—you are thoroughly encouraged to chase it. If you simply want to sit on the bench and paint your toenails black and read Neil Gaiman books, that's okay. (You will probably wind up being the person who becomes general manager of the Dodgers.)

Practice: Practices will be held once a week, for fifteen minutes, and they're optional. You might say, *Wow, that's not a lot of practice time.* And you are right. Coach and your parents are tired, they have errands to do, and let's not all get carried away with perfection. You guys are eleven.

Extra practice: No.

Score: We will ignore.

Wins/losses/standings: Also ignore.

Statistics: Chill.

Long bus trips: Absolutely not.

Game strategy: We will show up wearing pants.

Enthusiasm: Zen Cubs will stick up for Zen Cubs.

Always. We will cheer, we will clap, we will chuckle mildly—that's chuckle *with*, not *at*—okay, maybe it's a little bit *at*—when one of us runs to third base instead of first on a ground ball, but we will also pick each other up whenever someone catches a pop fly with his or her nose (and we will do that lots of times). We will scream when one of us hits a long fly ball to deep left field that looks like it's . . . okay, that's Coach's car.

Uniforms: Remember your pants. You can pretty much get away with forgetting everything as long as you bring your pants. (*Remember Your Pants,* incidentally, was the original title of *Little Victories.*)

Dogs allowed on field: Don't be ridiculous. Of course dogs are allowed on the field. Bring all the dogs. And the cat. Though the cat may be bored.

Turtle: Fine. The turtle too.

Daydreaming: The Zen Cubs have a very pro-daydreaming policy. Do not worry if your mind wanders while you're standing out there in right field. If a line drive sails your way and you miss it completely because you're thinking about what it would be like to eat a pizza ice cream sandwich, or if you're worried you didn't put Sprinkles the guinea pig back into the cage in Ms. Ferly's classroom earlier in the afternoon (you didn't, by the way), do not panic. (We will send the guinea pig to fetch the baseball. Tell Sprinkles to be careful and look out for the dogs and the cat.)

Substitution: All players, dogs, and the cat will play a

minimum of one game at every position rotating around the field. (The turtle will just play first base. Sprinkles will DH.)

Hitting the cutoff man: Not sure what this "cutoff man" is. Googling that right now.

Travel team: *Shhhhhhh.* Don't say it out loud. Freaks your parents out, makes them clammy and worried about how much time they'll be spending shuttling you around in the car this summer. I'll just level with you: Mom and Dad aren't totally jazzed about the travel team idea.

Parents: Parental participation is welcome *but by no means encouraged!* Parents are asked to deliver you to the games in a punctual fashion; they may bring water and orange slices, and perhaps a Maker's Mark for Coach, but they may not live vicariously through the ups and downs of the Zen Cubs. The Zen Cubs do not play for their personal amusement, to settle petty interparental feuds, or to realize their unrealized sports dream. They must not ask if you deserve more playing time, or if you could benefit from a two-week All-Star camp in Tallahassee, or if you "have what it takes." (We have no idea what it takes.) Parents may not climb a chain-link fence to threaten an umpire or tackle another parent in the parking lot and roll around over a disputed stolen base. Parents who cannot adhere to these basic and very reasonable requests will be BANNED from Zen Cubs activities and also forced to take Sprinkles the guinea pig home on weekends.

That's it. We're going to rethink the way we think

about sports. Test positive for seriousness and you will be suspended.

See you at the ball park. Nine-thirtyish, but don't hold me to it. And don't step on the turtle.

Your Friends at the Zen Cubs

P.S.: Pants.

★ The essential thing for all of us to remember about sports is this: they're games. As soon as we are able to stand on our own and play sports, a cheery phrase is repeated ad infinitum by adults: *It's only a game.* It sounds so good—just play the *game*, it's all for *fun*. Then we're dropped off at the field and abandoned to a stern-jawed coach who calls us by our last names and reminds us subtly (or not subtly) that it is in fact *sliiiiiightly* more than a game, that while we're all here to have a good time and run around and learn and be good teammates, it would be also nice (*very!*) if you helped the team, you know . . . well, maybe not explicitly *win*, but *not lose*. Many parents only compound the confusion, because they've put their lives on hold and spent money and driven kids around and they'd really prefer to *not lose* too, so they're hollering at players and coaches and referees and generally behaving as if they're on the verge of a motorcycle bar brawl. *It's only a game* shrinks as a group objective pretty early in the youth sports process, and it's a shame, because it denies the pleasure of the experience and replaces it with an absurd delusion. Here's the harsh truth: almost certainly you and no one with you is ever going to play a sport when it means something—like *really* means something, like livelihoods and incomes and business rely on it. Pretty much everything else is a *game*.

★ That is absolutely the best thing about sports. Fun without consequences, as the saying goes.

★ You appreciate this distinction more as you get older. Youth sports get poisoned with seriousness too early: the moments get magnified, the result becomes so achingly important, the losses are harder to take, the mistakes are overdramatized. *What more could I have done? What if I'd run a little harder? Why did that chubby squirrel run off with that ground ball?* When you're older, mowed down by a job and obligations and anxieties, and you get out and exercise for a little while, you tend not to sweat the box score so much. Win or lose, you're thrilled just because you got out of the house. You've exerted yourself physically, and think, *Now I can eat two doughnuts without hating myself!*

★ This is not to say there aren't adults who behave like lunatics when they get out onto the field or the court or the golf course. No matter how old you are, you will encounter the Serious Player. Serious Player wants to tee off from the pro tees. Serious Player just called an offensive foul in a pickup basketball game. Serious Player definitely says that lob was out even if Serious Player does not know whether that lob was out. Serious Player went to fantasy camp, has memorized his max and resting heart rate, and is wearing *compression shorts*. Related: Serious Player is three times divorced.

★ When I was little, I went to go find my dad at the public tennis courts down the street from our house—there was something I needed to tell him, and I was gabbing at him from behind the chain-link fence, surely being kidlike, loud and whiny, when a Serious Player on the court next to my dad hollered over, "Hey, would you mind telling that *kid* to *keep it down*?" And my dad suddenly wheeled from me, pivoted toward the Serious Player, and took a few menacing steps toward him, racket raised. "What, are you playing for your *mortgage*?" my father said. And though I had no idea what a mortgage was, my heart swelled immediately: my dad was defending me from strangers who had the audacity to complain about a kid during rec tennis.

★ I also have a lively version of this story in which my father chases the Serious Player around the court, swinging his tennis racket, but I am pretty certain that never happened.

★ Of course, seriousness has invaded nearly every aspect of sports, especially from the audience/consumer standpoint. We've stripped them of a lot of joy. Especially when I watch college football and basketball, I am immediately depressed by the cartoonish severity of it—the fuel injection of TV cash and national pressure; the wan, humorless coaches fetishized for bizarro work ethics and neglected families. (The college kids in the stands in painted bodies look like they're having a good time; everyone on the side-lines resembles an overworked heart surgeon at 3:00 A.M.) The pro game, meanwhile, has been neutered by its fealty to suite holders and corporate ticket buyers and a general tendency to gouge every aspect of the fan experience—$40 to park, $120 to sit down, $40 to drink, $18 if you dare to eat a hot dog and fries. It's natural that the individual who can afford to pay these prices regularly might be tuned out, a little too consumed by accoutrements and buffets, or smartphones, or the town car coming to fetch him in the seventh inning. This disengagement is embarrassing. Every time I see an empty seat behind home plate at Yankee Stadium, I want to permanently give it to a kid. Or a bunny rabbit.

★ Youth sports might be even crazier. Youth sports make me feel a thousand years old now. They're incredibly organized and professionalized and bear little in common with the youth sports I remember. I prefer a Little League team where three of the kids have forgotten their shoes, the second baseman might be asleep, and nobody plays left field. It's okay to be a little ragtag. It's okay to be the Zen Cubs. You should forget the score by the time you get to Mom's Toyota.

★ The Little League World Series freaks me out for this reason. First, the baseball teams are so incredibly talented and technically efficient—they hit the cutoff man. They in no way resemble the Little League of my youth. But now television coverage of the event has been grotesquely expanded to the earlier regional rounds, building up thirteen-year-olds before they even make it to the main event in Williamsport, Pennsylvania. Please know: as a kid I loved the Little League World Series—I would have sold my brother to the circus for the chance to play in one— but it is hard to not be turned off by all the adult business energy now committed to it. I have never understood why the TV booth at the LLWS is staffed by adults. If I ran the network, it would be three kids in blazers, eating chicken fingers, drinking Capri Suns, forgetting who's at the plate, and laughing at each other's farts.

★ We all had good and horrendous coaches. I had a youth soccer coach who, to his great personal entertainment and my teammates' confusion, would refer to me not as Jason Gay but as Jason Homosexual. I had a very kind Little League coach who arrived at practice one day and told us all he'd unlocked the secret to hitting: *while at the plate, close one of your eyes.* It took a pretty steady two weeks of getting plunked by pitches before he agreed that it might not be a wise approach. The same coach also drafted a notorious bully who had once yanked me off my bike and pummeled me near my house before a thrilled group of kids (the slugfest ended with his celebratory jumping up and down on my ten-speed until its basket was bent). It was the worst beating of my adolescence, and not long after, the culprit found me in the hallway at junior high and got in my face: *Guess what, I'm on your Little League team!* Fantastic. Happy to hear it. As it turned out, he was a great hitter and outfielder, and I kind of grew to like him. Fun fact: he's now serving a life sentence for murder. Aw, Little League memories!

★ Sports specialization is very bad; everyone seems to know this, and yet parents still believe in it, and kids are doing it more than ever. When I was growing up in the seventeenth century, a child migrated from sport to sport—a common pathway was soccer in the fall, basketball in the winter, and baseball in the spring. Somewhere along the line, it became modish to stop this flighty athleticism and specialize in a single sport. Today there's a huge industry built up to letting kids focus on one thing for twelve months of the year. You can't find an orthopedist on the planet who thinks obsessively playing baseball or basketball or anything year-round is a good idea—they believe it accounts for a lot of the repetitive-stress and Tommy John–type surgeries they've seen. If you talk to professional athletes, two things you're often struck by are 1) how few of them specialized and 2) how late they began playing their chosen sport. Some of them did not begin until junior or senior year of high school. Some even later.

★ If you ever get the opportunity to watch young athletes with a professional scout, take it. You learn very quickly that scouts evaluate talent a lot differently than we do. For example, the star of the team, the small but balletically coordinated kid racing up and down and making everyone else look bad? The scout is probably not interested in him or her—that kid has peaked. The awkward kid who is long-limbed and can't score and looks ready to fall asleep on the bench but had that one moment where he or she jumped four feet in the air? Yes. The scout would like a word.

★ When I am around elite professional athletes, I am always amused by how we've all agreed to forget what surreal miracles they are. Even the mediocre ones we complain about on sports radio—they're flukes from a long, illogical, near-impossible road we all once started on. Yes, these athletes work incredibly hard, and yes, they are dedicated, but making it to the pros is also a destruction of long odds. During a postgame interview, you just want to say to somebody playing pro basketball, *Do you realize you're playing pro basketball? Isn't that nuts?* The good players realize it's crazy. Roger Federer is like this. On occasion I've seen Federer at a press conference after a loss, and a question will come that suggests he should be morose, as if a train has just hit his dog, and Federer will grow a little snippy and fix the interrogator with a glare that says, *Do you realize what amazing good luck it is to be me?* And it is. (I like to imagine Federer saying everything while wearing a gold cape and petting an albino tiger.)

★ I am bracing for my own chapter as a sports parent. I hope I am restrained. I hope I maintain proper perspective. My dad's strategy for maintaining proper perspective was not going—I seldom saw him at a game, and if I did, he usually had his face buried in a book. I don't think that was bad or aloof parenting. I think my dad, a coach himself, was giving kid sports what he believed was absolutely the proper amount of attention, which, to him, was little attention at all. (My dad did, however, march onto a field during an *active Little League game* and yank me from the pitcher's mound—and he was not the coach of this team—after one particularly gruesome report card arrived in the mail.) I tell myself I will care the proper amount. I will never yell. I will never push. I will never walk my kids home after a game and relive a bad play or a missed opportunity. I will not live vicariously through their sports misadventures; I will not pick fights over playing time or peruse intense one-week off-season sports camps on the Internet. We will keep things amateur and loose. I will remind myself that there's almost a zero chance that my child or any child around will reach the professional stage, not to be a jerk but to dial down the obsession. I vacillate between telling myself that I will never coach and wanting to be the coach of a team that does things the right way, that doesn't care about wins and losses and prohibits obsessiveness and crazy parenting and sets an example for the rest of the league. I would take a team like that to the Little League World Series. We could just hang out in the parking lot and let the air out of the tires of the ESPN trucks. Maybe it's those Zen Cubs, happily anchored at the bottom of the standings, playing with no expectations, daydreaming at the plate, missing the cutoff, turtle in the outfield, playing a game like, you know, a game.

Travel and Snack Packs

I am an imperfect traveler. I know I want to travel, but I rarely feel like I get it right. I got a late start. I did not step on an airplane until I was nearly out of high school. I did not leave the United States, except to visit my dart-playing relatives in Canada, until I was thirty. By now I have been to the Winter Olympics in Russia and to South Africa for the finale of a World Cup, but I have yet to climb a mountain, take an ocean liner cruise, rescue a panda, ski behind a talking whale, or purchase that giant bottle of cologne in duty-free. I order the worst chicken dinner on every foreign menu, I forget to charge my phone or buy enough gum, and I *always* pick the wrong line to stand in at airport security. When I was young, my dad packed our family up in the Toyota and drove us across the country to California, but what I remember most is sitting in the back of the car, eating ham sandwiches and doing elaborate puppet shows for my brother. I think we also saw the Pacific Ocean. I spent most of my twenties broke and staring at the back page of the newspaper travel section, wondering if there was any way I could scrounge together $399 to fly to one of those all-inclusive resorts. If I ever got there, I vowed, I would eat so many ham sandwiches they would regret ever opening their fancy all-inclusive resort.

When I got a job in New York, I thought it was enough of a big deal that it warranted a celebration, and even though I remained broke, I bought myself a ticket to Florida and treated myself to a couple nights at a Ritz-Carlton. I thought this was something adults celebrating something did. I knew nothing about the Ritz except that 1) it was supposed to be classy and 2) my grandmother had been a telephone operator at the Ritz in Boston for many years. It was not a family tradition, however. When we walked past the Ritz in Boston, my father would hustle us down the sidewalk, worried that if we stood there too long, we might be handed a bill.

I calculated that I had enough money to cover the plane trip and the hotel room if I paid my credit card bill at precisely the right time. Anything else, I'd bleed into the red zone. If you've ever stayed in a swanky hotel, paying for "anything else" is the business model. Valet parking? $$$. Minibar? $$$$. Breakfast costs as much as a bicycle. Panicked, I scrambled off to a supermarket to buy water and stashes of Oscar Mayer Lunchables—simultaneously the planet's best and saddest foodstuffs—which served as my sustenance for the remainder of the trip. I lingered at the pool, trying not to sit or spend money. Guests at the Ritz were older and more advanced with careers and families and portfolios. I was a strange man eating cheese and crackers from a plastic bag.

I know that solo travel can be a spiritual journey, constructive for self-evaluation. This was not that. This was not Eat, Pray, Lunchables. I was lonely as hell, eager to get home. I learned this: I need travel with a purpose and a little action, or I get lost.

A few years later I was working at *GQ* magazine when I came across an item in a newspaper about a man in Minnesota who had discovered he was a Nigerian prince. No, not one of those princes who send an e-mail asking for the routing number to your checking account. This Minnesota guy, whose name was Marty, had been adopted at birth, and in his late thirties he began looking around for his birth parents. He learned that his mother had been a college student in Iowa who had met and fallen in love with a visiting student from Nigeria, who had returned to Africa before Marty was born. It took years for Marty to track him down, but it turned out his father was still alive and the chief of a rural village in southeastern Nigeria. This made Marty—a mortgage broker, father of two, basketball coach—a prince.

The newspaper story said that Marty hadn't yet been to Africa to visit his dad, and that he was hoping to raise enough money for the trip. I wrote to Marty, explained who I was, and asked him, if he ever figured out how to go to Africa, whether

I could possibly go along. It must have sounded like such a weird offer—*Care to share the most seismic event of your personal life with a random crackpot from a men's fashion magazine?* Weeks passed. Then one afternoon I got a clandestine call from Marty's wife: she had raised the money through friends and her church and they had purchased a round-trip ticket to Lagos, Nigeria. Marty was almost forty years old, and he was going to go find his dad. And they wanted the random crackpot from the men's fashion magazine to go along.

This was how I found myself weeks later on a rutted road thousands of miles or so from home, pressed into a raggedy Peugeot with Marty, Mark, a *GQ* photographer, and Mark's assistant, Luke. Mark was a celebrated photographer—he'd taken zillions of magazine covers, from Brad Pitt to the Stones to the cast of *Seinfeld* dressed as the cast of *The Wizard of Oz*—but he'd never been on a trip like this before. None of us had. We were essentially winging it. There were multiple legs to complete, madcap airports, chaotic roadways, and small bribes or "dashes" at checkpoints—you know, just the usual travel hiccups to watch someone find a father he'd never met before.

Marty was unruffled about the whole thing. He sat there in the passenger seat of the car wearing shorts and sandals and a T-shirt for a T.G.I. Friday's chili cook-off. He maintained a placid calm, as if he were on his way to a Twins doubleheader and not on the verge of having his whole perception of himself turned upside down. The Peugeot rambled over the dirt until we arrived in what appeared to be a village with an open grassy field in the middle. The car was swarmed by children, who began chasing us and slapping the doors.

He has come!

When we stepped out, a crush of children surrounded Marty. They were joined by adults, who we would soon learn were Marty's brothers and sisters (six of them!) as well as aunts and uncles. The crowd grabbed at Marty's T.G.I. Friday's chili cook-off T-shirt and yanked him toward the house, where a small, broad-shouldered man appeared in the doorway: Marty's father, Udeh-ekeh John Ogike. He moved slowly across the front porch and began to run his hand over Marty, inspecting him—arms, face, eyelids sleepy like his own. Marty recognized the resemblance and began to cry. And Udeh-ekeh began to cry too. He cried so much that another one of his sons, who hated to see his father upset, walked away and hid behind a car.

I spent two weeks there. I didn't want to leave. There were parties almost every night. Palm wine. Soccer in the field with kids from the village. One afternoon Mark assembled a family photo; everyone dressed in ceremonial clothing and the town gathered to watch. We were never alone. Toward the end of the trip I remember lying in bed at night—Marty was in another bed on the other side of the room, and he was talking about how blessed he felt to have come here, to be surrounded by this new family and meaning he'd never even considered. Rather than freaking him out, it calmed him. Back home in Minnesota, Marty had his job, his kids, his suburban life, but now there was all of this. This had not been my journey, but it was a perfect trip. At its best, travel is going somewhere else to find home.

★ We will all hereby agree that travel is important. Yes, yes, yes. Experiencing new places and people and cultures—whether next door or on the other side of the world—is a valuable life pursuit that nourishes the soul and results in a spectacular number of shot glasses purchased at airport gift shops. Do not ever stop! Go far away, visit places you've never seen, challenge yourself, learn new languages and how to drink at noon. However, there *are* times that "Travel!" starts to feel more like a guilt trip than a recommendation, and unless you're a college graduate trapped at a commencement ceremony, you're probably not in a mood to hear it. It's okay. Here's a tiny secret they don't tell you at your college commencement ceremony: sometimes adults just want to lie on the couch, eat mint chocolate chip ice cream straight from the container, and watch Goldie Hawn–Kurt Russell movies. That nourishes the soul too. No judging.

★ If you opt to stay at home, just don't call staying at home a "staycation." "Staycation" is just a fancy term somebody came up with for "I'm staying home to binge-watch *House of Cards* and finish a bunch of crap." If you ever hear a friend or family member refer to staying at home as a "staycation," you may slip outside and quietly let the air out of one of their car tires. Now it's really a staycation.

★ If you want to travel this planet far and wide, it's good to start doing that when you're young. This is not to say that the seniors among us can't travel the planet far and wide—since retiring, my mother has hopped around the earth like a secretary of state on Ritalin. It just gets harder to pull off the more complicated your life gets. If you have a job and a mortgage and three kids and travel soccer, you're not going to just *whatever* it to Prague on an open-ended plane ticket. But when you are young, you have a greater tolerance for travel inconvenience, scuttled plans, the occasional money shortage, and the Lady at the Place Who Can't Find the Key. You will sleep on the couch of a stranger. You will sell your sunglasses for breakfast. You will roll with it. The older you get, the harder it is to roll with it. At this point of my life I can't even roll with the Holiday Inn Express running out of cereal.

★ When Bessie was eighteen, she took a "gap year" between high school and college and traveled to Australia, where she adopted a pet rat, stood on a corner in downtown Sydney and window-washed cars—Bessie claims to have introduced the squeegee business to Sydney—and later joined a traveling circus in which she served as a horse groomer and an acrobat. When we're at a party and the conversation turns to Interesting Jobs We Had as Kids, my wife's arresting tale of crossing the Australian continent as a member of a traveling circus is like having Springsteen show up and sing "Rosalita." After that, nobody wants to hear about my stupid summer as a tennis instructor.

★ Ideally, travel should be a mixture of the familiar and the unfamiliar. If your family has a fifty-year tradition of rent-ing the same lake house with an ant colony in the bathtub and the same jar of orange marmalade in the fridge since the LBJ administration, stay with it! Traditions are useful, and so is the emotional balance of the expected, like that tattered edition of Monopoly with half the pieces missing. Balance travel tradition against the occasional unknown: not necessarily an exotic destination—you don't need to rent a tree house in the rainforest—but a trip that takes you out of your comfort zone and gives you that awkward but also invigorating feeling of dislocation by which you can actually lose yourself in something new. That doesn't have to be the other side of the world. It can be two towns over. It just has to break you from your routine. It would probably help if you didn't go to the Olive Garden two nights in a row.

★ By now we all know that tourist destinations tend to just replicate each other—it's as if cities don't trust their own histories and get worried that if tourists get off a bus and don't see a Starbucks and a Burger King within eleven seconds, they are going to get back on the bus home. A bunch of years ago, *Time Out New York* magazine did a hilarious story in which a reporter walked up to tourists in line at chain restaurants in the city and asked them if they'd be willing to try a nonchain restaurant, with the magazine coming along and footing the bill. *Hey, you like the Olive Garden? How about we take you to a real red-sauce place not far away that is seven hundred times more delicious, and pay for it?* And what I remember about that story is how difficult it was for the reporter to convince tourists to do it, as if he were an ax murderer trying to shove nice people in a van.

★ That said, I do miss some cheesy comforts when traveling. There are return flights home during which I genuinely fear I will barge past my wife and children at baggage claim and hug the pretzel guy behind the counter at Auntie Anne's.

★ If you are renting a car, there are two essential rituals. The first is the inevitable argument with your significant other about insurance, in which one of you (me) will want to reject insurance and put tremendous faith in the protection of a credit card you are still not sure you should have tremendous faith in, and the other person (not me) will want to buy so much insurance that it costs twice as much but you can basically return the car spray-painted bright orange and chopped into thirds and it won't cost you a dime.

★ The other ritual is that the person behind the counter will announce an exciting upgrade, and the upgrade is a PT Cruiser. Do not rent the PT Cruiser. It is billed as a "fun" car, and it is a fun car, if you are five years old. A PT Cruiser is the car equivalent of rainbow suspenders or those giant sunglasses with the year in them that people wear on New Year's Eve. It seems that at every rental counter in the country there are clerks trying to seduce you with a PT Cruiser. Just take the midsize sedan that makes you look like a graying detective.

★ Packing? Here's the golden rule of packing: you don't need that.

★ I mean it. Packing really is unpacking—it's more a process of deciding what you do not need. Learning this takes a little time. Mistakes. Realizing that you're never actually going to play tennis in Rome, so there's no need to fly your tennis racket across the Atlantic, with an entire kit of tennis wear. Overthinking is the bane of packing. There are people who pack for unexpected funerals on their honeymoon, snowfall in the Bahamas, emergency bowling pin juggling, because *you never know*. *I* know! You don't need that. You need one bathing suit. A single pair of shoes. A sweater, not sweaters. Consolidate your luggage accordingly. If you are used to traveling with two bags, you can surely get your life down to one. If you travel with three bags, you can also get it down to one. If you travel with more than four bags, stay home.

★ I am neutral on the topic of rolling vs. folding clothing (having done both), but I draw the line at those vacuum-pack plastic bags you load up and then *VAAAwoOOOoooooooosh* use a vacuum to suck out all the excess air. This seems like an excuse to jam more clothes inside your luggage. It also makes you look like Jerry Lewis fighting a jellyfish.

★ And we are not checking bags. That's right: unless we're spending a month in the Himalayas or running away from home, we're going carry-on. And we're going to fit the carry-on into the overhead compartment. We're not going to be those people who sweatily try to wrestle a carry-on into the compartment with a full line waiting behind, tiring and shouting, "BUT IT FIT THE LAST TIME. IT ALWAYS FITS. I KNOW IT FITS."

★ It doesn't fit.

★ One day I will launch my own airline called Air Uptight & Organized, which will come with an advance screening of all fliers on their packing ability. It's a billion-dollar idea. There will be a test. You will need to be able to enter and exit a plane in less than three minutes. Air Uptight & Organized will become the most popular airline in the world. We don't even have to fly anywhere, actually—we can just sit there on the tarmac in smug satisfaction.

★ Leaving for the airport is always a contentious negotiation. I arrive two hours early. This is more than enough for domestic, sufficient for international, gives you lots of time to get through even the worst security line (remember, I always pick the wrong line) and grab something to eat on the other side (remember, I've done away with checking a bag, so I've saved you at least twenty minutes there). My adventurous wife, on the other hand, simply deducts forty-five minutes from the flight departure time and assumes that a Formula 1 race-ready taxi driver, a flurry of good luck, and her name being called repeatedly over the loudspeaker will deliver her to her seat before they shut the cabin door.

★ Airport rage is unacceptable and dumb. People who work at airlines are *trained* to ignore your rage. Trust me, if curling up in the fetal position at Newark Liberty International and howling, "WHAT DO YOU MEEEEEEAN WE ARE DELAYED FOR A MECHANICAL PROBLEM, YOU SAID WE WOULD LEAVE THREE HOURS AGO" would lead to a mechanic suddenly springing into action, everyone would do it.

★ If you are going on a vacation with children, it's essential to remind yourself of one important detail: you are going on vacation with children. And a child does not wake up at 5:15 A.M., feel the salt air blowing, glance over at the clock, and think, *Whoa, I don't have to go to the office today. I'm just going to flip this pillow over, close my eyes, and sleep until ten.* Nope. That kid is up and out and wondering where breakfast is and who in the Caribbean is going to show *Sesame Street.* Kids do not crave tranquility. There's never been a kid in human history who has looked at an empty beach and said, *Wow, such an unblemished and relaxing shoreline.* It's just a dull beach, and they are going to walk as far as they can until they find a water slide with go-karts and trampolines.

★ When you travel with small children, you concede your edge. You are now a suboptimal traveler. A problem. People don't want to sit near you. If you walk onto an airplane with more than one child under five, the rest of the people on the plane look at you as if you're walking on with a herd of wet goats.

★ Kids will need outside food. So will you. As far as air-planes and food go, just surrender to the general agree-ment that airplane food has been horrible since the invention of the jet engine. (Don't believe that nonsense about haute dining during the "golden age of flying." Everything tasted great when you had eight Dewar's.) No "guest chef reimagining" is going to change the fact that airplane prime rib tastes like a fraternity house couch. I do, however, hold a certain affection for the trend toward snack packs, for which an airline might charge you $8 for the most astonishingly random collections of tiny food-stuffs ever assembled. *Excuse me, could I buy an overpriced cardboard box with two carrot sticks, rock candy, cream of corn, five grapes, an eye patch, gummy bears, an olive, a nose-hair clipper, a miniwaffle, a s'more, a horseshoe crab, a map of Helena, Montana, and a tiny wheel of Brie?*

★ The most important trip I ever took happened not long ago, but I didn't even know it was the most important trip until many months later. It was a family beach vacation. With my parents. If you had asked me a decade ago to go on a holiday beach vacation with my parents, I would have walked out the door and run into the woods, never to return. I spent a regrettable amount of my life thinking that there was no way a family vacation could actually be a vacation—to me, it was a task, something to get through and then drive home from as quickly as possible.

But not long ago my brother and I somehow worked up the idea that we should take our parents on vacation to the Bahamas, and to make it extra-complicated, we would go to a place where some of my wife's family would be. This was an anxious combination, a Cocktail of Fear. And yet somehow it worked—my parents had somehow converted from adversaries to the world's greatest babysit-ters, if you could just relax about the fact that the world's greatest babysitters would take their grandchildren to the ocean bar at 4:40 every afternoon. There were minor skirmishes, of course, but the families intertwined and the

Cocktail of Fear just evaporated, like so many minor panics. When I go back to my childhood house and see the photographs from that vacation on the wall—Mom on the beach with Jesse, Dad floating in the shallows with a scuba mask on—I realize that it was the last time we were all together as a family, happy, healthy, relaxed. A couple months later Dad was diagnosed. I wonder what took me so long to realize what a good idea this was, why I'd been so stubborn.

That was a great trip.

Office Heavens, Office Hells

This is what it's like to lose your job.

Somebody comes to see you. It's early. This is by design. They want to get it over with, before the day gets started, before you can settle in. They have a Plan. You don't know about the Plan, but they have known about the Plan for a while. They want to get the Plan over with, so they can move on and settle in with their day, return texts, go out for a mango smoothie at 10:35, and return to their computer and read that story about Ryan Gosling rescuing a beagle.

They find a quiet place and they tell you right away. There is no small talk. No weather, no American League standings, no *Good God, did you see* Game of Thrones *last night?*

This is what they say: *We're going to have to let you go.*

This is a polite way of putting it, but it's also accurate,

because it feels less like a door being slammed and more like somebody releasing a grip as you're dangling off a bridge. A minute ago you were sitting in a chair eating a cinnamon raisin bagel, starting to dig into your day, and now you are in free fall, a blur of panic rushing at you—*what does this mean, how did this happen, how am I going to pay the bills, what am I going to do next?*

Meanwhile the person who just vaporized your job is babbling about details of the split—severance, vacation, COBRA—and you are hearing none of it. It's just noise.

You want to lie down. When people lose their jobs in movies, they're always tipping over tables and throwing phones through windows and giving the entire room a brilliant, Oscar-winning F-you speech, in which they triumphantly promise to create a new company that will put this ungrateful dump out of business. In real life, you sit there frozen, incapable of summoning anger, much less an Aaron Sorkinesque soliloquy.

You're told it has nothing to do with your performance. But you don't *really* know, do you? This morning you came in to your job, and you thought you had a job.

This happened to me in 2008. I'd been working at *Rolling Stone* magazine for about eight months as the financial crisis unraveled and the economy cratered and advertising went *poof.* For weeks, very talented and hardworking people started getting canned all around me. Cardboard boxes were brought to desks; there were hugs and farewell e-mails and short, teary walks to the elevator. I kept my head down, but I felt secure. I thought it wasn't going to happen to me. I was new, but I had a pretty senior-level job, and people with jobs more senior than mine told me many times to relax, that there was nothing to fear, the worst of it was over and everything would soon be fine.

Then, just a week before Christmas, someone came to visit me first thing in the morning. *We're going to have to let you go.* I remember thinking it was a prank. I smiled and didn't get a smile back. *Rolling Stone* wasn't a perfect place—I had dreamed of working at the magazine ever since I was a kid, but by the time I got there, it felt more like a museum relic; its iconic owner, Jann Wenner, seemed pretty distrustful of anything that had happened after 1977—but it was a good job. I was proud of the stuff we'd done, enthusiastic about the future. I thought I was safe. They'd told me that I was safe. Again and again.

I wasn't safe.

In the panic, I attempted to rationalize it, spin it, make it seem not so bad. *This was happening everywhere! I was not alone!* I wasn't even alone at *Rolling Stone* that day—I was among a handful of employees the magazine swept out in a preholiday purge. But even though this kind of layoff was happening everywhere—literally thousands of people around the country were losing their jobs every day, banks were collapsing, John McCain was suspending his presidential campaign—it was hard not to let the moment brew into something hurtful and personal. A dull, sludgy feeling of humiliation crept in.

The rest of the morning was a haze. I was sent to a human resources–type office I'd never seen before, where I was asked to sign papers and agree to severance and basically forget the whole thing ever happened. It's simultaneously clinical and one of the most vivid moments of your life, and you are spending it with a stranger who just wants to see what's up on Perez Hilton.

Back at my desk, a cardboard box appeared. Time to pack and leave. Colleagues began gingerly to approach, saying *Dude* and *Why* and *I can't believe it*. I hugged people as if I were about to board a spaceship, never to return. Then I walked to the elevator and down to a hired car waiting on the street. This was a strange gesture: they'd just cannonballed my life, but they would give me a sweet ride home. I got in the car with the stupid cardboard box on my lap, and I sobbed.

When you lose your job, people tell you as a reflex that it's going to be the "best thing that's ever happened" to you. You get sick of this very fast. How is this possibly the best thing that's ever happened? At the time, Bessie and I were getting married in a couple of months, the economy was in free fall, magazines were closing by the shelf-full, never to return. I didn't want to go out, see anyone. I was so embarrassed.

I went to see my therapist, Doctor Gerry, where I focused on my feelings of shame. *I've been so wronged!* My layoff had been written about in the *New York Post. Everybody in town knows, Doctor Gerry!* I could feel it. I had been to a friend's holiday party a couple days after getting sacked, and I'd gotten out of there within minutes, dreading eye contact.

Doctor Gerry sat there at the other side of the room in his wool sweater and began talking in his low-medium voice.

"Do you mind if I tell you something?" he said.

This was always a big deal: Doctor Gerry wasn't a huge fan of telling me anything. I liked him very much—he was smart and comforting, and when I was bored I'd beg him to tell me about his craziest clients—but mostly his style was to nod, let me talk and reach my own conclusions, and then charge me the price of a lobster dinner for four.

"Okay."

"This is going to be blunt, but it's true."

"Okay."

"Nobody gives a shit."

Doctor Gerry argued that while being laid off may have been a seismic moment for me, to other people it was just Something That Happened. Sure, some people who knew me might have been briefly stunned or sympathetic or even titillated, and yes, some may have even gossiped about it to others, but it was quickly forgotten and pushed to the side in the daily crush of information. It wasn't an emergency to anybody but me. I thought of how quickly I'd forgotten this type of news when it happened to other people.

When you're starting out in the workforce, you can quickly become immersed and confuse your job with your life. There are times that I miss that kind of obsession—long nights out with coworkers after closings, the close attention to office battles, the comical pettiness of the usual workplace grievances. Hopefully, the pettiness declines as you get older and develop other, bigger, healthier obligations outside the office. We are many generations into the fetishization of work life, and while sacrifice and hard work are often essential, we have placed too much personal value on how we fit into a workplace. All of us want to make our work work. But we are not our jobs.

Doctor Gerry was 100 percent right. Nobody gave a shit.

I've never opened that stupid cardboard box.

. . .

★ I was also sacked from my first job. In my early teens I was hired by a man who lived a few miles from me to do some light landscaping, which included attending to the putting green he kept in his backyard. This putting green was his pride and joy. He owned a special weighted mower to do it, and on the first day he spent an hour showing me how to operate it. On the second day I yanked the blade too low and ripped a long strip of grass and dirt out of the middle of the green. His beloved putting green now had a terrifying jack-o'-lantern smile stretched across the middle of it. I thought he might weep. In the garage a short while later, he paid me and said, "I'm going to have to let you go." I said, "Okay, thank you, I'll see you tomorrow." I had no idea what "let you go" meant. He finally had to say, "No, I mean, don't come here tomorrow." I was too embarrassed to tell my parents. For a few weeks I would ride my bike off around the appointed time and then ride back home a couple hours later. Which was pretty George Costanza of me, thinking about it now.

★ All jobs become two jobs. The first job is your actual job—you know, the stuff you're actually supposed to do for the money they give you. That's the satisfying part. The second job is the role you play in the unspoken Broadway musical that is called *The Workplace*, and that role often has very little to do with the stuff you're supposed to be doing. Throughout your career you will encounter many drama-generating people who pay no attention whatsoever to the work but are virtuosos at the musical. They are masters of gossip and politicking and the maneuvering necessary to stay a step ahead of the chopping block. They are Jedis of sucking up, but they might not be sure how the workplace actually operates, and they are by far the least fun people to hang out with at the office holiday party.

★ If you're getting started on your career, know this: nobody expects anything from you early. Yes, occasionally you encounter a young person in his or her first job who is full of whimsy and vigor and feelings of wanting to overtake the world and own a jet at thirty. This kind of person may soon find himself or herself locked in a closet with the printer paper. Usually new people in the office are freaked out and intimidated by the mysteries of the workplace. If you are, please know you don't need to master it right away. If you are twenty-two and in a panic about where you are right now—relax. You're twenty-two. Sit down. You could go to jail for five years and half the office would not notice.

★ Don't go to jail.

★ By now we've all agreed that meetings are terrible, but occasionally they are a necessity. Lately there's been a shift to the standing meeting (*Look at us—we're all bored in the meeting, but we're standing!*) and the walking meeting (*We're bored but walking*) and even the super type-A running meeting, in which the sinewy boss summons staff for a satanic sunrise 5K. Forget that. I support one kind of meeting: the meeting right before lunch. Nobody wants to stay more than five minutes, nobody raises a hand, nobody tacks on extra business, because that really good taco place is about to open and *tacostacostacos*.

★ Everyone will have good bosses and bad bosses. The bad bosses make you briefly miserable but do give you plenty of material for funny stories over cocktails. I once rented mopeds at a moped shop owned by a boss who, when business was slow, took us to his home and made us wash all the windows in the house. But the good bosses stay with you always. My first great boss in newspapers was my first editor, Dick Reston, who gave me my first writing job and used to stand over me when I was typing, gently ashing his cigarette onto my shoulder as he edited my opening paragraph. There was my editor at the *Observer*, Peter Kaplan, who hired me after a bizarre double interview in which I bungled our first conversation and he asked me to walk around New York City until I had a better idea of what I really wanted to say. My editor at *GQ*, Jim Nelson, was endlessly curious and enthusiastic, whether it was about a story or about finding the most random restaurant in the most faraway city. My current editor at the *Journal*,

Sam Walker, basically took a chance on hiring me to write a goofy sports column and hoped I would not burn down his garage. The best bosses share a common characteristic: they are encouragers. It's easy to be an ass-kicker, to find the holes in someone's professional ability, but good bosses see a flicker of something and just let it barge out the front door.

★ Still, an underrated part of being a boss is maintaining order. You can't just let everything fly; they call you a boss for a reason. I had a boss who was beloved but could not discipline an employee, ever, which made that workplace a comforting environment to exist in, but it got to be a problem in terms of deadlines and inefficiencies. There was a rumor—never confirmed—that some of the more senior editors decided it would be a good idea to hire a paid actor to join the staff for a week. The actor would be grandly introduced at a staff meeting and then, at the end of the week, the boss who couldn't fire anybody would suddenly fire this paid actor for being a lousy employee. The boss who couldn't fire anybody would know this paid actor was not really an employee and could finish the job. It was a brilliant idea. This plan was scuttled at the last minute, word had it, because they didn't have money to pay an actor, although I like to think it was because the boss couldn't bring himself to fire the paid actor.

★ It's been a long time since I worked in an office every day—the *Journal* has allowed me to write from home as a free-range organic columnist—and there are certain things

I miss. I miss the conversations and the jokes and the easy shorthand that develops over sharing space and office nemeses. I definitely miss eating the goodbye cake for the coworkers I didn't really know. But the truth is I was a terrible office worker. I spent an astonishing amount of time talking and gossiping and involving myself in dramas that accomplished nothing. Now I'll be out somewhere with coworkers and it is briefly thrilling to hear the latest dirt—*Wow, did Geoff really expense a donkey?*—but you soon realize how useless and distracting it all is, how little of your time at work was actually time working.

★ Geoff did not expense a donkey. I'm pretty sure. If he did, it's filed under "Donkey Miscellaneous."

★ This is not to say there aren't plenty of distractions you can find working at home. Raise your hand if you spent an hour this week lying on the living room carpet taking close-up black-and-whites of the cat.

★ Just me?

★ Joining the company softball team is a nice way to meet coworkers and burn about six calories, but you need to make sure of what kind of company softball team it is. Is it the kind of team that takes itself seriously, wants to win, and imports ringers who have nothing to do with the company? Scamper away fast. You want to play for a company softball team that is excited but hasn't won since radio was invented and may smoke weed in the outfield. Typically the boss does not play for this type of team. Typically the boss could not name anybody on this team.

★ Do not feel bad about dreading the company holiday party! Everybody dreads the company holiday party. In fact, if you are excited about the company holiday party, this is likely a signal from the lighthouse to cancel, because you fit the profile of the person who winds up kissing four coworkers, then stands on a couch at 2:00 A.M. railing against the company health-care plan before passing out, then waking up twenty minutes later and demanding that everyone take you to Atlantic City for breakfast.

★ Somebody once taught me a brilliant holiday party strategy called "The Big Boss Grab and Go." It involves going into the holiday party, walking straight up to the boss, and having a pleasant ninety-second interaction in which you say just *one* memorable thing. It might be a joke. It might be a compliment that's about something other than the party (don't compliment the party—everyone compliments the party, and the party may actually be horrible). Walk right up to the boss and make eye contact, shake hands, and depart like you're Nicolas Cage walking away from an exploding van. Leave without saying goodbye to anybody, and be back in your bed watching *Downton Abbey* on Amazon by 8:45 P.M.

★ On the matter of workplace gifting: don't listen to anyone who tells you "gift up only" or "gift down." If you're the kind of person who describes coworkers as "up" or "down" relative to your own position, you probably deserve to fall down a modest-sized flight of stairs. If you are the kind of person who enjoys giving a gift, give it to the people at work who actually help you and deserve a gift. And then get one for your boss. Don't be an idiot.

★ Recently I have done a little bit of work on-air in television, a job that has its fun side but also transports you back to a very turbulent emotional place called the sixth grade. You suddenly become consumed not with your ability to speak and think fluently (which is supposed to be the job) but with how you look (which is mostly the job). You find yourself at the blunt end of physical criticisms you haven't experienced since teenage life. The standard complaint people on TV get is *How is this person on TV?* which you need to realize is mostly TV's fault, not your own, because TV has basically spent its existence trying to sell you a version of what a human being looks and sounds like which is not human or normal at all and is more like a handsome robot trying to sell you a condominium.

★ Advice for your next job: The first few years, don't say anything. Cultivate an air of detached mystery. Dress impeccably and open all doors. Attend all staff birthday parties and farewells and clap wildly at toasts. Once a month, dress completely in orange. Never send an e-mail. Stay late every Thursday, singing gently to yourself and pruning a bonsai at your desk. When it's Take Your Kid to Work Day, bring in a spider in a plastic box. Implement the 11:45 A.M. meeting. Take everyone to that really good taco place. You have my word: you will become an office legend and, pretty soon, the boss.

Gyms Are the Same

I am going to the gym. This time I really mean it. I'm going to make it happen. I'm going to stick to a plan. A *regimen*. That's what you call a plan when it's sweaty and life-affirming. A *regimen*. Because I am not getting in *shape*. Shape is what you have when you can climb four flights of stairs. I am achieving *fitness*. Fitness is what you have when you can sprint through a forest and hunt a pig with a spear. I am going to be fit. I am going to change my life.

(Okay, I am eating a taco right now.)

I am not an optimal gym-goer. I never have been. I commit and decommit. I whip myself into a frenzy and then let my interest quickly slag off. The excuses pile up. I'm too busy. I'm too distracted. I have children! I begin to rail haughtily against the very concept of a gym. *I'm not interested in spending my early-morning free time running in silence on a treadmill next to strangers. I am not a hamster.*

(I am having a second taco.)

And I really need to go. You don't understand. I really, really need to. It's been days. Weeks. Months. When I walk into the gym, they're going to treat me like I have found my way home from another dimension. My key card has probably expired. They've probably moved the elliptical machines to a new floor. Maybe the gym went out of business. The gym became a bank, and then the bank became a pet groomer.

Will I make it stick this time? I always have abundant theories, one crazier than the next.

It will stick if I work out early, in the darkness.

It will stick if I work out at lunch, like the skinny people in the office who come back to their desks with wet hair at one-thirty.

It will stick if I work out very late at night, after midnight, a solitary figure doing bicep curls in a window.

I will join a gym that is 5 miles away, and I will run there, work out, and then run back. I have calculated how many calories I will burn if I do that six days a week. I could eat three whole pizzas for breakfast.

I will buy new gym clothes, which are elastic and neon and contoured to my body and have some odor-eating magic dust that makes them not smell like rat garbage. These clothes will make me feel like I'm a first-round draft pick. I will pack them in my gym bag. I read about that somewhere: I need a gym bag, which will carry only gym-specific items, and I will not put my gym items in a briefcase with a nine-day-old ham sandwich, three adapters to computers I no longer own, and a sweater I've been meaning to return to J.Crew since 2009.

The clothes and the bag will confer a degree of seriousness before I even set foot in the gym. And I'm really going to set foot in the gym.

(I am having a third taco.)

I'm going to do all of this. This is happening. When I walk in, I am going to sign up for classes immediately. None of this "go at my own pace" nonsense. I know where "go at my own pace" goes. It goes to Dunkin' Donuts.

I'm going to take the hardest classes with the strictest teachers and I am going to stand in the front of the class. I am not going to stand in the back where I know I can hide and look at my smartphone when I'm supposed to be doing burpees. I'm not supposed to look at my smartphone during burpees. Does Tom Cruise look at his smartphone during burpees? No. (I believe Tom Cruise has his assistant look at his smartphone during his burpees, and if Tom Cruise has to take the call, his assistant does the burpees.)

I'm going to take that really hard class, that tough one that meets at 4:15 A.M. Mondays, Wednesdays, and Fridays where everyone has to climb a tree carrying two gasoline cans filled with sand. I'm going to take that class where everyone learns to do a one-handed handstand. I'm going to take the class with the wild-armed instructor who can't stop excitedly playing "Walking on Sunshine" as if it came out two days ago. I'm going to be the person who sits next to you at dinner and can't stop talking about my workout. I'm going to wave away dessert as if someone is passing around poison.

You will not like me. But I will like me.

I'm going to jump rope. Single unders, double unders. I'm going to dead-lift, squat, row, focus on my form. I'm not going to look in the mirror, because I am not in this for vanity. I'm in it for the long-term health. It's not a fad, or something I'll quit after twelve days or the first time someone offers me truffle fries. I am done with truffle fries. The next time you see me you're going to say there's something different and you can't quite place it.

It's a life overhaul and it starts today. This is going to change everything.

But first I'm going to have a taco.

. . .

★ I love it when people say the problem with your gym is that you haven't been to the *right* gym. Please: I've been to the right gym. And the wrong gym. I've been to the cheap gym, the fancy gym, the gym that had a lobby that looked like it belonged to a sheik, and the gym where I was afraid to sit down anywhere. I've belonged to a gym where a nice man handed you a clean workout outfit every day—not a workout towel, but a workout *outfit*—and a gym that had a bar serving smoothies. There have been gyms that smelled like Paris in April and gyms that stank like some-one left a deer head in the trunk of a Corolla. I've been to the spartan gym too, the one where they throw you in a cold corner and ask you to lift a concrete block as a mouse runs by, points at you, and laughs. I've been to the old-school gym, the old-old-old-school gym, and the gym that claimed, very loudly, in commercial signage, that it was not like any other gym.

Nope. The gym that was not like any other gym was like every other gym.

I have been to enough gyms to have concluded that it's all one big gym. Some gyms might spend a lot on accoutrements, and some do not, but it's essentially the same routine. The gyms that don't spend a lot on accoutrements like to make a big deal about their refusal to do so, as if it's a religion, as if you're a jerk if you want, say, air conditioning or a bathroom that doesn't look like it's behind the wheelhouse of a lobster boat. There's usually a front desk, there's machines and lockers, and there's always one Stair-Master that doesn't work—it's actually a rule, every gym on the planet must have a StairMaster that doesn't work. It just sits there, hoping someday to be repaired or converted into a coral reef. There's the good spinning instructor and the bad spinning instructor, and there's a guy who comes in every day at 2:00 P.M. and bench-presses in his jeans for ten minutes and leaves. Every gym has that guy. He's ripped and kind of amazing.

★ Every gym also has a copy of *Us Weekly* that is seven years old and has been read 35,000 times and at this point could survive a nuclear attack. There's an article in it about Courteney Cox that is surprisingly moving.

★ You know the PERSONAL LOCKS ON LOCKERS WILL BE CUT AT END OF NIGHT sign that exists in every gym locker room? This is just a ruse, a scare, and it never happens. They never cut locks. There's a locker over there that has had a lock on it since 1987; it could have a mummy and a stolen Rembrandt inside.

★ Hotel gyms are almost universally terrible. Every once in a while you encounter a handsome hotel gym, where the machines all work and there's a TV tuned to CNBC and a pitcher of ice water with persimmon and orange slices, which tastes so good, you swear that when you get home you're going to start drinking ice water with persimmon and orange slices, which of course you never do. But most hotel gyms are dumps and dungeons. They tend to be on the first floor or in the basement. They have one window, which looks out onto an alley with garbage cans and the occasional homicide. They look like the kind of room you get sent to if you've stolen socks at Macy's. Still, you have to use a key card to get in there, because the hotel does not want you, you know, ripping them off and walking out with a 2,800-pound rock-climbing machine. There is never anybody in the hotel gym, ever. Until the moment you arrive, when a traveling businessman in his khakis walks in right behind you and begins to roll around on the floor with an exercise ball while watching CNBC. He'll be there for six hours, and may or may not be a guest at the hotel.

★ I'm not the biggest fan of watching television while working out, but when I do, it has to be the most mind-numbing television possible. I want Kardashians buying their valets parakeets or ESPN's *First Take* debating

Gatorade baths or the cast of a local news morning show arguing over the best way to eat a gingerbread house. I can't handle anything slightly serious, that requires even the mildest concentration. I do not want to pay attention. A terrible basketball game is perfect. I think the most perfect thing would be breaking live CNN coverage of an eighteen-wheeler that has gently tipped over, releasing a trailer full of kittens chasing bouncing Super Balls. That's about right.

★ Personal trainers can be great, but a good personal trainer should get on your nerves a little bit. Your trainer should be friendly but not your friend. He or she should push you in ways you don't want to be pushed. Like that friend who is always urging you to watch that documentary about wind power, a personal trainer should make you do things you wouldn't otherwise do. Not crazy push-your-limits stuff, just making you dead-lift three more reps than you ordinarily would dead-lift. Those three extra reps are often the difference between getting fit and farting off. A trainer who is a little bit grating isn't necessarily a bad thing. During a good personal training session, you should want to punch your personal trainer a few times.

★ Do not punch your personal trainer. You will regret that.

★ By now you have surely heard the phrase "There is no workout that can outrun bad nutrition." This was not true when I was nineteen, when I could eat a bag of cheddar and sour cream Ruffles for breakfast and not gain an ounce, but it is definitely true now. Today when I eat a syrup-drenched waffle, I *become* a syrup-drenched waffle. On the flip side, food is fuel, and you do need to eat. You cannot have three almonds for breakfast and think you're going to tear it up in spinning class. You will ride six minutes and need to lie down.

★ I have made my peace with spinning class. As someone who has ridden a bike for a long time, I had a hard time adapting to spinning—I found a lot of it unnatural and unspeakably goofy, full of a lot of unnecessary movement and odd claims about rpm's and body positioning. I'd go to a spinning class and do my own thing—I'd resist the calls to bounce up and down, and I'd sit in the back like a Bartleby the Spinner, pedaling comfortably at 90 rpm. (Basically I was a jerk.) The mistake I was making was viewing spinning as a simulation of cycling. It is not. Spinning is no more a simulation of cycling than playing chess is a simulation of eating chocolate cake. Once I was able to accept this separation, I began to enjoy spinning for what it was, which was a reasonably solid workout and an opportunity for me to hear Pointer Sisters songs I'd completely forgotten.

★ I did CrossFit for a while and I won't lie: I really enjoyed it. CrossFit is easy to make fun of—it happens in "boxes" that look like abandoned auto garages (because sometimes they are) and people do old-fashioned exercises as if they're in prison yards and they pull their socks up high like your grandpa going to the pharmacy. CrossFit is a little bit faddish, but so what: it works. What I most liked about CrossFit is that it teaches you all the stuff you're too intimidated to do in a gym. The instructors get you to do it correctly, and nobody makes a big deal if you can't even bench-press the September issue of *Vogue*. CrossFit thrives on its no-jerks ethos, which can be a little difficult if you're, you know, a jerk. I credit CrossFit with getting me strong to the point that I could do five pull-ups, which I put slightly before the birth of my children and the time I found a kiosk selling iced coffee in the Moscow airport as the happiest days of my life.

★ The true secret to fitness? I'm convinced it's this: doing anything physical repeatedly. *Anything.* You don't have to belong to a gym or wear special clothes or even psych yourself up as you get ready in the morning. There is no magic class or formula—it's all the grind of repetition. People who walk three miles to work in the Himalayas do not think, *Oh, man, if I could just get to SoulCycle, I could lose these love handles.* Because they do not have love handles. (They also do not have 7-Elevens.) Anything done all the time—it works. This is not to say that walking on a treadmill and watching *Real Housewives of Atlanta* is the same thing as competing in a three-week Tour de France. But commitment is the only science that matters. It's the breakdown of commitment that fuels the carnival of optimism and failure that is the gym industrial complex.

(It's also the tacos.)

Thanksgiving and the Touch Football Game

Several years ago we had an idea at the *Journal* to do a column about the rules of Thanksgiving family touch football. At the time I was just desperate for a column. Then, weirdly, happily, it turned into a thing. People read the Thanksgiving Rules column, passed it around, disagreed with it, posted it on Facebook, offered their own rules. Readers started sending in photographs of their own family touch football games—whole clans posed in the backyard, looking as if they had just rolled around in the rosebushes. (Sometimes they sent in the score.) In 2014 we got Bruce Arians of the Arizona Cardinals—a real-live NFL head coach—to diagram a special touch football play. To this day, the Thanksgiving column is the column people ask me about. Or yell at me about.

TEN KEY RULES FOR THE
THANKSGIVING TOUCH FOOTBALL GAME

1. Your touch football game must take place before Thanksgiving dinner. Trust me: nobody in your family wants to play touch football after dinner. After dinner, everyone in your family wants to put on sweatpants and fall asleep watching a terrible NFL game.

2. Keep the touch football field much smaller than you think. Not regulation size—are you kidding? If that field is more than 40 yards long, six people in your family are going to wind up on oxygen in the hospital.

3. There are really two plays in touch football: go out short for a pass and go deep for a pass. Be careful about who you send out deep. If you make your Uncle Lou go out deep, Uncle Lou is going to need a few minutes to sit down in the back of his Lincoln.

4. How dare you sack your mother? That wonderful woman drove you to swimming lessons for six years and also let you watch *Beverly Hills Cop* when you were twelve.

5. Do not bring cleats or gloves or anything that gives the impression you were prepared for a family touch football game. If you show up in eye-black and an authentic NFL jersey, everyone is allowed ten minutes to point and laugh.

6. If you wear a blazer and tie to Thanksgiving, you will definitely be the first person pushed in the mud.

7. If you are new to the family and you catch three TD

passes, you need to start dropping a few on purpose, or you'll be promptly driven to the bus station and never invited back.

8. Yes, your aunt is drinking wine and eating crackers in the backfield. It's okay. She also ran back an interception for a touchdown. So back off.

9. The halftime show? The halftime show is Dad drinking a bourbon on the porch and complaining about the neighbor who hung up his Christmas lights in the middle of September.

10. No whining, taunting, or sobbing in Thanksgiving touch football. That's what Thanksgiving dinner is for.

. . .

I enjoy Thanksgiving. Almost all of it. I like that it's a food-based holiday; I like that you're not expected to bring a present; I like any day where it's okay to fall asleep at 4:15 P.M. I like the cranberry sauce everyone says is natural, and also the canned cranberry lump that looks like a robot's kidney. Of course Thanksgiving usually involves spending hours with extended family, and spending time with family can be treacherous—everyone has wanted to spend a Thanksgiving or two hiding beneath an upstairs bed. There are always food crises and travel hassles and strange guests and plenty of listless TV football. But it is an American ritual, and we are stuck with it. You can elope, you can drop out of college, you can ignore your children's birthdays, but you're on the hook for Thanksgiving.

★ In the months leading up, everybody mulls over two different versions of Thanksgiving: a version of Thanksgiving in which they spend time with their family and all the emotional turbulence that entails, and, conversely, a blissful version of Thanksgiving in which they skip the family turbulence and spend the holiday with close friends who don't give them a hard time.

★ Let me get it out of the way: you're not spending Thanksgiving with your friends. That only happens in movies and prison.

★ If you have to travel for Thanksgiving, there's no magic secret. It's all horrible. The roads are congested, the airplanes are overbooked, the trains are delayed, and somebody just walked onto the bus carrying a tub of gravy. Of course, you can take the bus in August and someone will walk on carrying a tub of gravy. That's what happens on the bus.

★ Do not leave your mother in the lurch in your Thanksgiving plans. Your mother wants two things in life: she would like you to stay in touch and she would like the Thanksgiving plan to be ironed out at least eight weeks in advance, preferably ten. (Mom would also like someone to explain why she can't download more than two movies on her iPad, but good luck on that.)

★ There will be some discussion about whether you should stay in your family's house or just get a hotel. The hotel is completely worth it: it will give you some freedom and the ability to escape any family craziness, in the end making you fresher, happier, and better to be around. But sorry, you are staying at the house.

★ Nobody likes a visiting turkeyologist. A visiting turkeyologist is the person who, upon arrival in the host's kitchen, begins to propose an alternative cooking strategy for the turkey, based on a careful reading of a magazine article he or she perused on the train. The visiting turkeyologist expresses suspicion that the host's turkey will be cooked to its potential and begins fussing with the oven. It is okay to stash this person in the garage until dinner is served.

★ Be careful about kitchen experiments. Everyone remembers the Thanksgiving when Uncle Steve was really excited to cook the turkey in the smoker and the whole family wound up having bowtie pasta instead.

★ Hovering and stealing food is an expected ritual of Thanksgiving, but proper kitchen hovering and food stealing must be executed under the cover of a dutifully performed kitchen assignment. If you are peeling potatoes, nobody will notice that you just ate 2 pounds of stuffing.

★ Don't spoil your dinner by eating all the cheese and drinking all the vodka.

★ Of course, too much vodka and by three o'clock you might be jumping on the dining room table and telling everyone in the family what you really think of them.

★ There are at least two relatives who make "_____'s famous" dishes. A "_____'s famous dish" is a dish this relative has been making for fourteen years and nobody has the heart to tell him or her to stop bringing it. It is almost always cooked with a can of beer and at least one Snickers bar.

★ We are running out of people on this planet who know what they are doing with mashed potatoes. It's a major cultural issue, like the decline of horse racing and clock-making.

★ Nobody gets much credit for making turnips either, but turnips are the offensive line of Thanksgiving. You think you don't really need them, but try to get through a full Thanksgiving without turnips.

★ Be sure to hide all your Valium, because your cousins are coming and they know where it was last year.

★ Sure, make a healthy salad, but you know . . . it's Thanksgiving. Let's not get carried away.

★ Thanksgiving dinner will not start on time. Thanksgiving dinner always runs about ninety minutes behind, like a Prince concert.

★ Actually, that is pretty good for a Prince concert.

★ Thanksgiving is definitely a time when a lot of people like to break out the "good" china. If you have such a thing as "good" china, I am going to assume there is not a lot of talk about farting at your Thanksgiving table.

★ Every family remembers that year when Mom had a hip replacement and Dad panicked and moved Thanksgiving to that restaurant with the buffet and the chocolate fountain. You're supposed to act like you didn't enjoy that Thanksgiving because it wasn't at home, but everyone secretly loved it and wished it happened every year.

★ When dinner finally begins, many families like to say grace. This is a time to give thanks for your health and your loved ones, and that your sister finally broke up with that married squash coach.

★ Thanksgiving dinner never looks or sounds like it does in the cinema. The fights are never as dramatic, the turkey is 50 percent less glamorous, and nobody's dad resembles Craig T. Nelson.

★ When Craig T. Nelson was born, did he just look like somebody's dad?

★ If someone at your Thanksgiving did the 8:00 A.M. town Turkey Trot, you are never going to hear the end of it.

★ A Thanksgiving paradox: you will spend your entire childhood trying to get to the adult table and then all of your adult life trying to get back to the kids' table. When you're a kid, you don't realize how much the kids' table rocks. You can sit down when you want, and there's not a lot of emphasis on table manners or even eating your whole plate, and usually there's been enough worry that you won't eat enough that someone just drops a whole pizza in the middle of the table. Stop me when any of this sounds bad. (Up until the early '80s, kids could smoke cigarettes at the kids' table.)

★ You can unbutton at the table, but please be discreet. One button. Two or more buttons may wind up being forgotten and end up poorly for you in family photos.

★ By now even the trainers have given up instructing people to take it easy at Thanksgiving. They know it's a lost cause. The problem is you have three slices of pie, and then it becomes a habit, and then you have a twenty-three-slices-of-pie-a-week problem and are robbing pie stores to get more pie.

★ You have an aunt who is feeding an imaginary dog under the table.

★ A good old-fashioned political screaming match can be very lively and just the spark your dinner needs. If you are so stubborn in your political opinions that you shout everyone down, you are ready to run for president.

★ Yes, we saw your new car outside. No, we're not asking you about it.

★ You need to have at least one new person at your Thanksgiving dinner every year. It is not this person's job to cook or clean. It is his or her job, however, to have his or her life picked apart like an alien abductee's.

★ If you are the new person at somebody else's Thanksgiving, it is your job to have a very colorful life and romantic escapades. If you do not have a colorful life or romantic escapades, make some of them up. There's a good chance nobody has watched *Mad About You* in years, so you can just use plotlines from that.

★ The neighbor who comes over and says, "I'm just staying for a drink" and then stays for the entire Thanksgiving dinner? That was his plan all along.

★ Late in the dinner, grandmothers like to have another cocktail and go over the year in family wakes and funerals.

★ My brother, Chris, has always been a master of the sneak-away nap. He would pull out of dinner early, maybe twenty-five minutes in, citing fatigue, and then uncork a solid hour nap, returning in time for dessert, perfectly timed.

★ The proper amount of space between the end of Thanksgiving dinner and dessert is thirty minutes. Anything longer than thirty minutes, your guests will fall asleep or drive back home to North Carolina.

★ In my family there was always a polite hesitation about turning on the television for the football game. Like, to surrender to the NFL would be an admission of family dysfunction or our inability to generate compelling family conversation. Every year, however, my Uncle Ken would finally turn on the football game and we'd all rush in there like sheep. Shout out to Uncle Ken: thank you.

★ Those families who send photos from the Caribbean of their Caribbean Thanksgiving? Everybody loathes them.

★ In recent years it has become popular for some retailers to begin their Black Friday sales on Thursday night. Do not support this inane trend. If you feel like you want to replicate the experience, blindfold yourself, tape $150 to your forehead and roll yourself down a hill in a shopping cart.

★ When dinner is over you *maaaaay* have to watch some kids perform a Thanksgiving play. It's great! (Okay, the play is terrible but only about eight minutes long, so try to hang in there.)

★ If you are going to invite children to perform an impromptu postdinner concert, please consider what kind of music they've been practicing lately. If one of the children just began accordion lessons, slip off to the backyard.

★ You think nobody notices that you're not doing dishes; they totally notice that you're not doing dishes.

★ There are people who will happily wash dishes but are "pan shy": they don't want to muscle down and do the hard, greasy work with the pans. Don't be pan shy. Get your elbows in there and rustle around. Don't say, "I'm just going to let it soak." If somebody says, "I'm just going to let this pan soak," they will not set foot in the kitchen for two and a half years.

★ There's a really hard-to-scrub pan that sits in the bottom of the sink longer than any other pan. The person who cleans this pan will marry one of your siblings within eighteen months.

★ At a certain point all the kids under ten will go upstairs to watch three minutes of *Finding Nemo* followed by the entirety of *Amityville Horror II* and *III*.

★ If fewer than three people cry, it isn't a real family Thanksgiving, and you have to start over.

Your Phone Is Not You

A *Little Victories* quiz for you: Have you become too technologically dependent?

1. You are reading this copy of Little Victories *how:*
   a) As an actual hardcover book, with printed pages, by candlelight, in a hayloft, above sleeping livestock, as people used to do in the 1990s. *(0 points)*
   b) On a portable reading tablet I found in the back of an airplane seat twenty minutes ago when I was trying to hide gum wrappers and a potato chip bag. Is there any John Grisham on this thing? *(2 points)*
   c) What makes you think I am reading *Little Victories*? *(4 points)*
   d) What is reading? *(8 points)*

2. *You are attending an important business meeting. Under what circumstances will you check your phone?*

    a) Never. It's obnoxious and an affront to other people in the meeting. *(0 points)*

    b) That's rude. I never check my phone first in a meeting. I wait until somebody else does, then I check my phone. *(2 points)*

    c) I am in prison. But don't worry! I have an iPhone 6. *(4 points)*

    d) What was that? Sorry. I was checking my phone in an important business meeting. *(8 points)*

3. *What is a reasonable amount of time to allow yourself to spend on Facebook each night?*

    a) We have a firm family policy: no Facebook after dinner. Instead we work on exciting puzzles of springtime scenes in Holland, which we will do until our kids become old enough to run away from home. *(0 points)*

    b) Maybe a half hour? Trying to connect with my cousin Maartje—I need to ask her about springtime in Holland. *(2 points)*

    c) Haven't gotten on Facebook since Mom posted that video of herself dancing. *(4 points)*

    d) Sorry to ask again: is there any John Grisham on this thing? *(8 points)*

4. What is the longest period in the past twelve months you have spent apart from your smartphone?

    a) During my quintuple-bypass surgery two hours ago. *(2 points)*

    b) Accidentally left cell phone in car when I went to see my kid's school performance of *The Sound of Music*. Panicking, I decided to yank the school fire alarm during "My Favorite Things" and recovered phone from the passenger seat in time for the second act. *(4 points)*

    c) Answering this question is the longest I've spent away from my smartphone in the past twelve months. *(6 points)*

    d) Which *one* of my smartphones? *(8 points)*

5. What's the most embarrassing place you've asked for the Wi-Fi password?

    a) Amazon (the rainforest, not the online retailer). *(0 points)*

    b) Grand Canyon. *(2 points)*

    c) Nana's funeral. *(4 points)*

    d) I'm at Nana's funeral in the Grand Canyon. *(8 points)*

6. What's an example of technology going too far?

    a) Any kind of government spying. (Hi, government.) *(0 points)*

    b) Robot professors. *(2 points)*

    c) I'm a robot professor. That's offensive. *(4 points)*

    d) Dad favoriting you on Twitter. *(8 points)*

7. What technological advancement are you most looking forward to?

    a) Not looking forward to any technological advancement. I'm just going on a hike up this country hill at the predawn hour to watch this life-affirming sunrise. *(0 points)*

    b) A self-driving car . . . with a wood-burning pizza oven. Aren't those supposed to be here in a year? *(2 points)*

    c) Robot professors. *(4 points)*

    d) iSunrise. *(8 points)*

8. What piece of modern technology could you comfortably live without?

    a) Anything. Take your pick. No machine controls me. *(0 points)*

    b) My 1983 tabletop Ms. Pac-Man. Actually, please don't take that. I live alone. Do you think that is related to the tabletop Ms. Pac-Man? *(2 points)*

    c) Ryan Seacrest. *(4 points)*

    d) Children. *(8 points)*

ANSWER KEY: *0–10 points: Congratulations, you lead a balanced and relatively technology-independent life. 11–22 points: You have some dependency but you have things reasonably under control. 22–36 points: I'll wait until you're finished with that text. 36–64 points: You're never going to finish that text, are you?*

. . .

★ A few years ago, weary from work and eager to embark on some technological unplugging, I went on a three-day vacation in Mexico. By myself. My wife was on a trip to Africa with fellow teachers, visiting a sister school in a Samburu village in Kenya. I was buying tequila at the Cancún airport. My destination was Tulum, a beach town we'd visited a few times before, which prides itself on its earthy, low-tech vibe—there's not a ton of electricity; power is mostly by generator; it's tacky to walk into the hotels and ask about "the Wi-Fi situation." The whole point is you're supposed to unplug, sit on a chair, maybe boogie-board a bit, buy some mango from the guy who wanders up and down the beach every ninety minutes, fall asleep, and repeat this four times a day. Even though it's been invaded lately by hipster ding-dongs, I still can't wait to go. I had no big plans. I wanted to sit in a chair and drink Don Julio and read a book I'd wanted to read for a while: Sammy Hagar's autobiography.

For the first day or so, the lack of technology—or any human interaction—was a welcome breeze. I didn't have any newspaper obligations, and I couldn't even get my phone to work. Bessie was in Africa and unreachable. I was untethering in the way all those magazine articles about technological untethering told me to untether. My brain began slowing down. My eyes were noticing things they seldom noticed. I didn't miss Twitter or Facebook or sports scores or Internet photographs of cats pretending to play musical instruments.

But on the second morning I was sitting there in the hotel's little outdoor beach kitchen, with its small gas stove and its cute green lizards scrambling on the countertop, and another guest looked at me conspiratorially and said, "You know, if you take your phone over *there*"—and he pointed at a tree off in the distance beside the sandy driveway—"you can get a reliably great signal." I laughed, and ignored this advice for the rest of my vacation. What I meant to say is that I ignored this advice for about half an hour. Not long after my kitchen conversation, I walked out to the driveway and over to the specified tree, where I held my phone in the air as if I were the Statue of Liberty and started feeling a wave of e-mail vibrations. You know the scene in every drug movie when the drug addict who's been good at staying clean breaks down and uses in a highway rest stop? That's what it felt like. Sleazy and great and awful all at once.

When I brought the phone to my eyes, the first e-mail was from my boss:

"TIM TEBOW TRADED TO JETS. CAN YOU WRITE?"

That was the end of my three-day unplugged vacation.

★ It is strange/funny/depressing to think Tim Tebow being traded to the Jets was actually a big enough deal at the time that anyone would halt a vacation. Tebow never started a single game for the Jets. It's like saying you were late to the birth of your first child because Maroon 5 released a new single.

★ I'd argue that the most absurd aspect of our technology obsessiveness is that you wind up throwing about 90 percent of it out. Every piece of tech you use is destined to become a piece of tech you no longer use, far faster than you think. Your Walkman yielded to your Discman which yielded to an iPod that you once showed off like a newborn and now sits at the bottom of a basket filled with running shoes and dog toys. The navigation system in your brother's car, which looked amazing nine years ago, now resembles Pong on the dashboard. Your iPhone 1 is trash. Your iPhone 3 is trash. Readers and tablets and pads of all kinds are discarded and ignored. Angry Birds! Remember how bonkers you were with Angry Birds, how flying chicks and exploding pigs ruled your life? The proper way to use and appreciate technology is to recognize that it all becomes disposable and useless, like razors and college diplomas.

★ I had a cell phone before any of my friends did. Somehow I convinced my dad it would be a good idea. You know, for safety. He was not an easily persuaded man, but for some reason he bought both my rationale and the phone. It was a flat Nokia about as big as meatball sub and had a long antenna you pulled out manually. My father gave two strict commandments when he gave it to me: 1) *Use the phone only in case of an emergency* and 2) *Don't ever use the phone*. "It costs ten dollars a minute," he howled. My dad was prone to hyperbole, and I had no idea if this was true, but I would run through scenarios in my mind:

Upside down in a snowy car accident on an abandoned road, pinned against the steering wheel, fumbling around with my one free hand on the driver's side, locating the phone, pulling out the antenna with my teeth, dialing 911, I suddenly have a vision of my enraged father opening up a bill for a $400 phone call. Basically I owned an unusable nonsense phone.

Still, I was proud of my unusable nonsense phone. I took it with me everywhere, grandly depositing it on whatever table was in front of me, waiting for a reaction. And the reaction was not always awe. We forget, but back then cell phones were not considered a modern necessity. They were a symbol of ridiculous self-importance—a statement that your reachability was essential to the functioning of the universe. *Oooooooooh, a cell phone. Mr. Faaaancy! Are you going to take us to your* yacht? friends would say. I would flimsily defend my ownership. I didn't need it. And by and large, I still don't need it. It's just not something you need to defend, because everyone has a phone now, to the point that the haughty thing is to not own a cell phone. Seriously: tell people you don't have a cell phone, and the reaction is the same: *Ooooooooh, no cell phone! Mr. Faaaancy!*

★ My friend Josh grew up in New York City in the '80s and led an extraordinarily active social life and likes to point out how extraordinary social lives were possible long before people started carrying around phones. You simply made a plan and kept it. Pay phones were utilized.

Answering machines. Sometimes your roommate took
a message and wrote it down by hand, like a hieroglyph
of a buffalo on a cave wall. This crude system somehow
worked. People were late, people didn't show up, sometimes the roommate failed to write down or remember
the message, but we were not consumed by the real-time
whereabouts of our friends. And you didn't miss anywhere
near as much as you'd think you'd miss. "In all those
years," Josh likes to say, "I missed only one party." (It
was a St. Patrick's Day party; he realized it when he got
home and checked his answering machine.) Whenever I'm
scrambling somewhere, texting thirty times to organize a
single dinner, I think of Josh and his one missed party.

★ If you have young children, you know it is impossible for
them not to be drawn to and completely fascinated by
a smartphone. And yet if you hand a child a phone in a
public setting, people look at you like you've just given
your kid a sack of enriched uranium. You are lazy, you are
ceding parenthood to the machines, you are not actively
building organic fun. The parenting magazines and blogs
tell you to set limits, and this is useful advice, but I am not
setting limits on, say, an airplane. If it means a peaceful
cross-country flight without dirty stares from every other
passenger, I will let a two-year-old watch *Scarface*.

★ I am active on social media—that phrase just sounds
weird, like my mother talking about a new exercise
class—and I continue to have a hard time understanding
all the hatred on social media. I don't mean the predict-

able critical hatred—*your album sucks, your book sucks, this book sucks*—I mean the truly hateful, derogatory, racist, misogynist, useless, and hurtful agitation that is epidemic in many corners of the Internet. It seems like such a fearful and futile waste. In theory, the Internet provides an opportunity to widen knowledge—to see beyond screens and neighborhoods into a broader universe—and yet the first thing many people want to do is wall themselves off and broadcast how narrow-minded they are. It seems to absolutely miss the point of the experience. It's like buying a bike and throwing it immediately off a bridge.

What's obvious is that so much of the agitation on the Internet is redirected loneliness. Social media offers an opportunity for instant reaction, and that reaction, like any intoxicant, is both euphoric and dangerous. You can become reliant on it, and when it goes away, it can make you sad, angry, depressed—and inclined to lash out. So much of the anger seems to be born of that kind of disillusionment. And it serves no broader purpose. The handful of times I've found myself in stupid Twitter frays I have thought, *Nobody is paying me to do this. I immerse myself in this crap for free*. I brought it on myself, voluntarily, like someone who lets a drunk horse into his living room. And I do not want a drunk horse in my living room. Maybe later, but not now.

★ I believe in being nice on the Internet as a smart, counterintuitive strategy. Nice may not be as visceral or as immediately exciting as mean, but nice does separate you from the fray. That is the thing about being an asshole on the Internet: *that job is taken!* There's too much competition. There are a lot of assholes doing it better, more fiercely and meaner than you do, and you're going to have to get in a very long line. Nice, by contrast, has openings. Nice takes you someplace. Nice is a lifestyle and a business.

★ This why I have a hard time getting too worked up about affirmation culture on places like Facebook, Twitter, and Instagram. Yes: I have taken embarrassing personal satisfaction in having mundane Twitter observations retweeted by strangers. Yes, it is maddening when my wife posts a photograph of a real-time event we are currently experiencing and then checks every five minutes to see how many people have liked it. The approval-seeking aspect of social media is slightly desultory, but it's still a currency of niceness. It's not ruining days. Sure, you may be lying when you say my kid looks "Cute!" when I post a photograph of him eating beet salad, when it actually looks like he's blood-soaked from eating a live pigeon. But it's okay. It's nice of you.

★ A few times when I've received some particularly hateful comments from people, I've taken the time to reach out to them via e-mail—and a couple of times phone calls—and say hello. And I mean "Hello!"—I'm not trying to be confrontational. I simply say who I am and say I read what they wrote and say I regret their disappointment. The reaction is almost always surprise and backpedaling—you can hear the smoke screeching off their tires. Then the apologies commence. I don't need an apology. I just think a lot of people view the Internet as this place where rudeness doesn't stick, where the usual decorum of human interaction isn't necessary and even the most incendiary language isn't really real. I think it's useful to remind people every once in a while that it's real. It's also kind of fun.

★ Technology is rushing to reduce the routine of everyday human contact, the assumption that human contact is, you know, a pain. Anything that verges on a person-to-person experience is now considered extraneous, worthy of streamlining, if not total elimination. Why pay the cabdriver cash when you can use a card? Why use a card when you can use a phone? Why take the cab when you can take a car? Why take out your card when your card can simply be automatically billed to your phone? It's gotten to the point where I no longer want to *call a restaurant* to order takeout food. This feels like a Rubicon of laziness. I'm already too lazy to make myself dinner or go out to eat dinner, and now I am too lazy to dial a handful of numbers on my phone and have a real human conversation. I find myself annoyed when I have to take a receipt or sign a bill. At the moment New York is awash in smartphone apps that promise alternatives to hailing a taxi. *Hailing a taxi!* We are not taking about building a log cabin in the backyard. We're talking about walking outside onto any avenue and *raising your arm.*

★ Still, I think the biggest hazard of technology is how it is pulling us away from the present. I see this all the time at sporting events: people who are sitting very close to the action—courtside, even—who are not watching the game and are instead consumed by their phones. Some of them are surely using the phone to broadcast their location: *At the Knicks, they don't stink so bad when you are up this close, suckers!* Technology makes a dubious promise of something better and fresher than where you currently are. We have theorized for a long time about the pursuit of "virtual reality" and what life will be like when it happens, but smartphones have already built a virtual reality apart from the present. (Disclaimer: I am not saying you need to pay attention to Knicks games, because in fairness they tend to be pretty disturbing.)

★ Working the newspaper business, you get a little tired of all the technological doomsday-ism, of people saying, *Wow, how's THAT business?* as if you're opening a restaurant for dinosaurs or selling T-shirts that say *Happy New Year 1993.* It's true that publishing right now is a bizarre mixture of resignation and anxiety. But it's coupled with the happy reality that so much of what you're doing is part of the everyday conversation. The mediums are changing rapidly—and thrillingly—but news isn't going out of business any more than sunshine is going out of business. Okay: TED Talk over.

★ Not long ago I subscribed to one of those "productivity analyzers" that measures how much time you spend—or don't spend—actually working on the things you're supposed to be working on. You tell the analyzer what programs/applications you use that are work-related (say, your word processor, maybe the dictionary, or a search engine like Google) and things that are not (Twitter, Facebook, basically every other thing on the Internet), and at the end of each week it sends you a spreadsheet of how you are doing, how productive you are being with your time. The results were terrifying. It was as if I had asked someone to film my sleep and then discovered that in what I *thought* was a reasonably sound sleep, I was wandering into the kitchen and eating 358 roast beef sandwiches. According to the program, my productivity rate was a little more than 50 percent. Keep in mind that I was writing somewhere between three and five columns a week for the *Journal* and I was still somehow screwing off 47 percent of the time. The analyzer then allows you to block certain applications/programs from your computer so you can eliminate distractions and raise your productivity. It doesn't completely eliminate your ability to find the Internet and mess around, it just makes it a hassle. It's the Homemade French Fries Theory, which holds that if every time you want French fries you have to buy potatoes, wash potatoes, clean potatoes, cut potatoes, and cook potatoes, you will eat a lot fewer French fries. And it has made me a more productive person.

I did not say happier. I just said more productive.

★ I would like French fries right now, enough to call and order them on a phone from a real person.

★ I don't think at this point it's reasonable to completely divorce yourself from technology. Are there people who do it? Sure. Are these people annoying? Sure. These magic smartphones and other devices have stuck their claws into our central nervous systems and have become intractable parts of our lives. There are surely opportunities for all of us to rely on them less. We don't have to check Twitter before bed. We don't have to watch all of *Battlestar Galactica* again. But I don't think it's embarrassing to recognize the occasional wonderment.

When my dad was sick and we couldn't be with him in Boston, we fell into a routine of doing a goodnight video chat with him at Jesse's bedtime. The ritual was a little ridiculous: Dad gaunt and exhausted on his TV couch at home, eyelids falling, dropping in and out of sleep; Jesse bouncing in his crib, barely able to stand still, much less focus on his fading grandfather in the tiny little window.

And yet this interaction briefly made us whole. We craved it. My dad craved it. It made me grateful to live in a time when this was possible, when this little phone could offer my son a brief flicker of facial interaction with a grandfather who wouldn't be here much longer. *What did people do before this kind of thing was possible?* It felt like a small miracle. But I realize now that the phone didn't make us happy. The moment did. The technology offered a beautiful opportunity, but the happiness was being in the moment.

I Dine at 5:45 P.M.

★ I am probably not in the proper life place right now to offer food advice. At the moment there are a pair of small children wailing away in my chaotic home. For the past two years I have eaten somewhere around 80 percent of my meals standing up. I subsist mostly on scraps left behind by a toddler. I eat chicken fingers, mac 'n' cheese, and broccoli treats shaped like dinosaurs, and drink from boxes of apple juice, and I can finish an entire sleeve of animal crackers during an episode of *Bob the Builder*.

When I walk down the street, I look inside the windows of restaurants with a kind of envious Dickensian glare. *I was once one of those people*, lingering over dessert and cappuccinos, talking about bands and *Broad City*. I was once one of those people, reckless, impulsive, living on the edge, eating after 5:45 P.M.

★ Like many families, we are trying to stay devoted to the family meal. You may have seen that the family meal has made a Great American Comeback. When I was growing up, the frantic mealtime hustle was a sign of progress—commercials depicted high-speed breakfasts in which Dad drank his coffee in the shower and kids on their way out the door to school caught minipancakes in their mouths. At dinner Mom popped a pizza into the micro-wave and handed it over to the clan in front of the TV couch. Family dinners? We were busy getting life done! Now there is a backlash to the hurried dinner. Now there is a return to the long, sit-down family meal, with a well-considered recipe, handpicked ingredients, and, good Lord, conversation. Partly this is a revolt against the mod-ern rush. Partly it's a desire to make a family connection. It's also a new appreciation of home-cooked food. It's what I want. It's what my wife wants. Also, microwaved pizza is horrendous.

★ But let's be real: sometimes the family meal is too difficult. Sometimes I think my favorite family meal is the one in which we talk about making an elaborate home-cooked family meal and then give up and order Chinese food.

★ I'm also not completely convinced that the home-cooked meal creates an essential bond between parents and chil-dren. When you were a kid, nothing was better than when your parents gave up and ordered—not microwaved—pizza. You never thought, *This pizza is nice, but it would have been better for our family dynamic to have a slow-cooked meal.* No, you thought, *Pizza!*

★ Early in the life of your family, you need to decide whether you are the family that stops at McDonald's or the family that has McDonald's at home.

★ Nobody has McDonald's at home.

★ At this point in my dad life I should have a handle on how to grill, but I don't. It's always a panic. I'm never like that dad in the commercial with eighteen hamburgers and two T-bone steaks and a dozen sweet sausages and hot dogs, sipping a beer by the pool. I feel I am okay with hot dogs and sausage and semireliable with burgers and steak. Chicken, I might as well be doing open-heart surgery. I am so afraid of poisoning you that I will leave that chicken on the grill until 2042. I do like standing around the grill, however. And in all the years I have been standing around grills, with many people of different ages and experiences—some truly distinguished in the art of grilling—do you know what the most common topic of conversation has been? How to grill the corn.

★ I want that to be on my tombstone: *I Never Totally Figured Out How to Grill Corn.*

★ Having people over to dinner? Here is the ideal number of dinner guests, including the host or hosts: seven. You say six or eight, I say seven. Why? Because an odd number helps. Even-numbered dinners invariably become gatherings of couples, and here's what's interesting about a dinner that's exclusively couples: *zero.* Unless you want to spend the entire night talking about real estate and the lice breakout in the sixth grade, invite an unattached spare, who will be picked apart at the table like a med school cadaver, making for hours of easy entertainment at his or her personal expense.

★ Anything bigger than nine guests, it's a football banquet and you need to invite everyone's parents and hand out awards and scholarships.

★ There's always one guest who eats 70 percent of the cheese. That guest is me.

★ No seating chart, psychopath.

★ No soundtrack either, psychopath. Just put some Adele on Pandora and calm down.

★ Serve salad before dinner, not after. What is this, Iceland?

★ Guests like to hear a little about the food, but that's about it. If you are complimented on the duck, tell your guests where you got the duck. Do not tell them where the duck went to college.

★ The duck went to Wesleyan, FWIW.

★ Keep the TV chitchat to a minimum. If you've discussed *Homeland* for more than forty minutes, lean into the table and set fire to your hair.

★ When the dinner party migrates from the table to the couch, the dinner party is over. Nobody is about to break out cocaine and put on Prince's *1999*. Two people are going to fall asleep right there, and if you don't call a taxi, they'll be there when you wake up the next day, eating your Froot Loops.

. . .

New York is a renowned restaurant city, but restaurants here can also drive you nuts. Food has been a sport here for many decades, but lately the mania has been ratcheted to the point where chefs are celebrities on a par with athletes and rock stars and restaurant openings are greeted with the fanfare once reserved for King Tut's sarcophagus. What should be a happy ritual—eating!—has been turned into a *Lord of the Flies*–style competition that can leave a person (me!) very insecure. It has reached such an extreme that at the moment there are websites that are effectively scalping tables to New York restaurants.

Table of four? *Sure, buddy. I can get you in. Partial unobstructed view of the men's room toilet.*

On the occasions when I have been lucky enough to find myself in one of these white-hot establishments, I have gotten crabby about a few things:

★ Waiting at the bar. I know a restaurant's reservation system is a flawed, evolving, fickle beast, and I know that when I arrive on time for an eight o'clock reservation, it is not always possible to be seated at eight o'clock. I get it. But I do not want to wait at the bar. The bar is crowded and everyone is standing and shoving forward to order $18 drinks and I just took someone's handbag to the ear. I am going to stand outside and talk to neighborhood dogs about the Stanley Cup.

★ Complicated menus. I promise to be a very polite and generous customer. But I would love ordering dinner to require less instruction than removing the engines from a 747.

★ Loud restaurants that confuse a shrieking racket with popularity and jam tiny tables closely next to each other like it's a high school chess tournament.

★ Please God, no more restaurant DJs. (No offense, restaurant DJs.)

. . .

I read in the *New York Times* that food mania has trickled down to people in their early twenties; people fresh out of college are now spending half their rent checks at the best new restaurants, which have become a social priority among young New Yorkers, like seeing a great band or throwing up on your roommate's futon. There is something about this that leaves me depressed. I don't have any objection to anyone liking good food, but it doesn't seem like it should be a focus when you're twenty-three. Locking yourself out of your apartment and having to kick your way in through the fire escape at 4:15 A.M. should be a priority when you're twenty-three. You will have the whole of the rest of your life to sit in good restaurants pretending to enjoy squab.

. . .

Restaurant jobs I have had:
1. Dishwasher.
2. Prep cook.

3. Dessert guy. (Scooped ice cream, cut pies, ate pies.)
4. Grilled cheese guy.
5. Morning cleanup guy (Pizzeria Uno, Madison, Wisconsin).

Best of these jobs? Dishwasher. There's no question. If you've been a dishwasher, you know what I mean. You're in the engine room. You're essential. The chef can flip his lid and walk out the door and the kitchen will figure out a way to cover, but the dishwasher is the glue. Everyone's nice to you; the waiters check in with you; the chef makes sure you get fed. There are loads of prima donnas in restaurants, but there's never been a prima donna dishwasher. You have to put your elbows down and get it done. At the end of the night, the dishes eventually stop, and there's a great feeling of pride and accomplishment, diminished only slightly by the fact that it's 1:00 A.M. and you smell like pickles and barbecue.

Worst job: You would think it would be cleaning up a Pizzeria Uno on weekend mornings, which was indeed horrible, and involved mopping up things that aren't supposed to be found on the floors of restaurants, but it was really my very brief career as a grilled cheese station guy. It was a grilled cheese station at a college dorm kitchen where I'd been washing dishes. I thought the grilled cheese station would be a step up, I really did, but it wasn't. I should clarify that this was the *nighttime* grilled cheese station. During the dinner shift I'd stand behind this counter and wait for kids to order grilled cheese sandwiches. Here's who orders a grilled cheese sandwich in a dorm: everybody. A grilled cheese is a backup plan against any culinary failure, because it is pretty impossible to mess up a grilled cheese. College students order grilled cheeses just because they're bored. And so I would make 21 billion grilled cheese sandwiches, lathering the bread in butter, waiting by the grill for the sandwiches to finish, flipping them onto plates, and developing grilled-cheese carpal tunnel. It took many years for me to come back to grilled cheese. But I am back. I love you, grilled cheese.

· · ·

Have you ever done a juice cleanse? If you haven't, here's what a juice cleanse is: you go to the juice store, buy somewhere between six and eight cold-pressed juices, the clerk charges you $85, and the staff laughs uproariously and high-fives each other as you walk out. Juicing used to be the domain of actors and vain billionaires scared by a brush with mortality. Now it's available to morons like you and me.

You never feel healthier than you do leaving the juice store. *You are really doing it!* You're grabbing your body and shaking it and saying, "It's time for a spring cleaning, buddy!" You have read all the vapid testimonials. Within days your skin is going to glow like Princess Grace's on a cruise to San Lorenzo. Your gut will look like a corner suite at the Four Seasons. Your tongue will turn a color it hasn't been since you were in pre-kindergarten. You will be gripped with enough energy to kick-box your way through an ultra-marathon.

Or something like that. Juicing has never seemed like a terribly practical or scientific endeavor, except for the part where you're consuming fewer calories than you would have if you'd gone to, say, Taco Bell six times a day. I've found it helpful in that it does seem to press a reset button if you've been punishing your body with empty junk. But I've never had a juicing epiphany. I've never experienced the Glow. My tongue is the same color it's always been: tongue. The biggest benefit seems to be just motoring through to the other side. I've managed three days and five days. I hear if you can do ten, it's pretty great. If you can do a whole month, you get X-ray vision and abdominals like Willem Dafoe's and can climb a coconut tree like a lemur.

. . .

People ask me all the time what the best thing to eat at a sporting event is, and I tell them it hasn't changed since your grandpa went to watch DiMaggio on the Yankees: a hot dog and a beer. I know stadiums are getting better with food now—there are sushi bars and minitacos and sliders, and if you hunt carefully you might be able to find a salad—but let me explain something to you: you're at a stadium. If you witness sports history, it should not be while picking at a salad. *Fisk's home run hit the left-field foul pole and Dad nearly spilled all his spring lettuce mix!*

. . .

Years ago my wife and I were on vacation in Florence, Italy, and like anyone vacationing in Italy, we were fanatical about making sure we were eating at the best places. No tourist traps, no chains, no places that made us look like suckers. The first night we asked the hotel concierge for a recommendation, and as we assumed was his job obligation, he recommended the hotel's restaurant, which he said was excellent and romantic and utterly worth our time. No thanks. We weren't falling for that. We hadn't come all the way to Italy to eat in the hotel restaurant. So he recommended another place, a short walk away. We waited in line for a half hour, and as we were about to go in, a departing American couple looked at us and made the puke sign as they were walking to the street. When I see strangers exiting a restaurant and making the puke sign to me, it scares me off. I am no longer interested. I am conservative like that. And so we walked around on our own and tried to find something, which is always a bad idea, to the point where we were hungry and snapping at each other, when we came across this low-lit restaurant that appeared to have a secret entrance in a stone wall. The place was on the Arno River, and it looked like a vision of what a Tuscan restaurant should be: romantic, cozy, almost clandestine. Amazingly, a table was available out on a balcony overlooking the river. We couldn't believe our luck.

Bessie and I proceeded to have what we considered—and still consider—the most romantic dinner of our lives. A lot of the joy was in the surprise of it—we'd been so close to pathetically packing it in for the night, and here we were, in one of the most beautiful places we'd ever seen, having a fantastic meal. And when dessert was finished and we paid the check, we walked away from our table and couldn't help but notice something we hadn't noticed walking in: the interior of the restaurant was somewhat familiar. We kept on walking until we reached another familiar space, and then the . . . concierge's desk. We had walked around Florence in circles for long enough that we'd wound up walking in through an alternate entrance and eaten at the restaurant in our hotel.

Good food isn't supposed to be hard work. If you're lucky, it may even find you.

Dressing Like a Dad

I don't consider myself to be an especially stylish person—or a slob. I dress somewhere in the middle. I am not the most rakish man at the wedding, but at least I'm better than your Uncle Brian, wearing his Jimmy Buffett *It's Five O'Clock Somewhere* T-shirt in church. I do not resemble one of those gentlemen you see in magazines, effortlessly pulling off a three-piece suit, a bespoke shirt rakishly unbuttoned past the second button, a leather monk-strapped shoe placed atop a luggage trunk—not a *bag* but a *trunk,* suitable for a transatlantic voyage. I do not look like that. I look like a guy who put on his nice shirt to go to the dentist. I do not dress up for the train, my birthday, or the movies, and when my wife tells me to put on a sweater for the holiday cocktail at her dad's, I kick an imaginary aluminum can. I wear shorts in October, sweats at midday, and proper shoes maybe ten times a year. Maybe five times. For long-distance flights I dress like I am on my way to a fourth-grade sleepover.

Still, I don't reject the idea that style matters. It's wrong to believe that fashion is frivolous; if someone is allowed to set money on fire buying Browns season tickets, I can accept someone setting money on fire spending $50 on a T-shirt. I too like to feel stylish, and sometimes I can allow myself the illusion that I actually know what I am doing. I believe there's some benefit: a confidence both internal and projected. The designer Tom Ford has said that a suit is a form of armor, that when a man is well dressed, it provides an aura of invincibility that helps get him through the day. I am with Tom Ford on that, though I know I am not well-dressed enough to be Tom Ford's cable guy.

I care enough to look like I care enough. I know I will never be confused with Clooney in Venice, but I do not want to look like a man who ran out onto the street because the meth lab was on fire. I spent more than five years working at *GQ;* some of it had to stick. I own a not insignificant number of blazers. I like tweed. I will wear a tie for no good reason. If this is starting to sound like bragging, I also spent the majority of the Super Bowl in 2014 walking around the press box with chocolate frosting all over my tie. Nobody said a thing. Yes, I cleaned the tie by licking off the frosting—don't be insane.

. . .

As I've gotten older I've realized that I am somewhere between being stylistically together and stylistically a mess. I'm a type, actually. Nobody likes to think they're a type, that they belong to any declared fashion subset—it diminishes individuality and makes it seem like individual choice is not a choice. But I'm okay with admitting that I belong to a familiar subset: the Slightly Exhausted Hipster Idiot Dad. We are everywhere, a cliché unto ourselves, easy to ridicule and recognize. You can find us staring at smartphones on playgrounds and soccer sidelines, or spending too long looking at the beer in the supermarket. All our clothes are a shade too tight for our flabby dad bodies, because we are vain, believe that we will return to being ripped like we were at twenty-three, believe we are not ready to wear relaxed-fit jeans. Even if we are *completely* ready for relaxed-fit jeans. Even if relaxed-fit jeans would make us somewhere between 40 and 50 percent happier. The Slightly Exhausted Hipster Idiot Dad has a haircut that cost more than eight bucks, a haircut that the Hipster Idiot Dad actually thought about before sitting in the barber's chair. It might not even be a barber. It might be a *salon*. The Slightly Exhausted Hipster Idiot Dad cares a little too much about sneakers. We own more than three hooded sweatshirts. There are at least two T-shirts in the closet that we have hung on to for twenty years and love as much as our children. One is an R.E.M. T-shirt. Neither fits (flab). When the Slightly Exhausted Hipster Idiot Dad has to prepare for a Big Night Out, it usually involves jeans and the Good Collared Shirt. The Good Collared Shirt lives in a slightly less occupied part of the closet. It is reasonably flattering and has been complimented at least once by a stranger. The Slightly Exhausted Hipster Idiot Dad's wife likes it. Or at least tolerates it. There is also a stain on the front pocket that may or may not be hummus, but the

Slightly Exhausted Hipster Idiot Dad is at least 70 percent sure nobody can see it. This is not true. Everyone can see it.

The Slightly Exhausted Hipster Idiot Dad is representative of fatigue, not surrender. He is at least one stage before Giving Up. Giving Up is sweats with no underpants to the airport. Giving Up is going to your mother's house on Christmas Day in a Dolphins jersey.

I am not there. Yet. But a Dolphins jersey sounds pretty comfortable.

★ During a twelve-month stretch between 2012 and 2013, I didn't buy any new clothes. For a year. As a test. One day I looked in my closet and saw the billowing piles of T-shirts and sweaters and realized, *This is cuckoo. I don't need this.* I gave a lot of clothes away. I did not buy anything in stores or online. Okay, that is not totally true: I bought a pair of tennis shorts. I bought a winter hat at the Super Bowl. But that was pretty much it. It was a liberation. It is amazing how much time frees up when you do not have to shop for clothes. You could learn to play a musical instrument in the time you spend shopping for and buying clothes. I did not learn to play a musical instrument. I farted around. When I wanted to wear something "new," I would dig into that overstuffed closet and find something I'd completely forgotten I owned. I am telling you right now: 20 percent of what's in your closet is things you have forgotten you own. It's like getting a new wardrobe you don't have to pay for.

When the year was up, I went back to old habits. I'm back to being a disaster. I buy things I don't need online. I buy sweatshirts for my sweatshirts, like I am concerned that my sweatshirts need friends.

★ I have even grown to love the Waiting Chair. Everyone has sat in the Waiting Chair watching somebody else—usually a spouse—shop. There should be a coffee-table book dedicated to Waiting Chairs all over the planet. But I wonder if my appreciation of the Waiting Chair is completely tied to the invention of the smartphone. I don't even remember the Waiting Chair before the smartphone. What did people do in the Waiting Chair before they could go onto e-mail and Facebook and text and play Temple Run? Did they just *sit there* in the Waiting Chair? Think? Be alone with their thoughts? Count the rivets in the ceiling of Anthropologie?

★ When you have a kid, it is your first opportunity to dress someone else, unless you are a stylist or one of those controlling lunatics who lays out your partner's clothes on the bed. Kids' clothes are astonishingly current and cool today. By four months, your child will be dressing better than you do. This does not change for the rest of your life.

★ A word about cargo pants. Society says you are supposed to stop wearing cargo pants as soon as you graduate from college and *maaaaaybe* one summer bopping around Copenhagen with a long-tailed white rat living in one of the side pockets. I still wear cargo pants, however. I like them and I don't care if people think the pockets are full of bong water. My wife chooses to ignore them, as if we're living in a Cheever story and the cargo pants are a secret family I have in Westport, Connecticut.

★ I am okay with logos, but I don't like those sports T-shirts that say stuff like *Let's Sweat* and *It's Biceps Time* and *Second Place Is for Llamas*. Nike has made a national affliction of these. I am okay if you want to tell everyone you went to Middlebury or the Grand Canyon or you like the oysters at the Little Oyster Hut, but I don't want a shirt to make an announcement about my athleticism or my tenacity or my intention to sweat all over you. Plus the directives seem to be going in the wrong direction. Aren't you supposed to be motivating yourself?

★ I may have come up with *Second Place Is for Llamas* on my own, and truthfully, I would wear that.

★ Conversely, I'm a fan of Accomplishment Wear from athletic achievements, whether it's a T-shirt signaling participation in a 5K or a New Year's Day plunge or one of those obstacle courses in which you crawl under barbed wire and ex-commandos shout mean things about your mother and your 401K. I refuse to pooh-pooh Accomplishment Wear. I support anything that encourages people to be active. You crawled over the finish of the Towson Turkey Trot after drinking five old-fashioneds the night before? Good for you. I'm awestruck and proud of you.

★ If you have to ask, "Do I look good in this cowboy hat?" please do not wear a cowboy hat.

★ On a visit home, my brother bought a Harvard sweatshirt as sort of a joke, since neither of us was close to Harvard material. But I wore it a couple times and it was an odd experience. It's sort of flaunty in the wrong ways. You wear a Wisconsin sweatshirt and people are kind of like, "Hey, Badger"—it's totally harmless and unbraggy, like telling people you like picnic tables and kegs. But a Harvard sweatshirt sends a different message. It's like walking into a room and saying, *Hey, I am very smart* or *My parents know people*. I felt like I was going to get pulled over by the campus police or hired to write for a late-night comedy show.

★ As a sportswriter, I am very familiar with the great American ritual of wearing a sports jersey to a football game, and I have made my peace with it. I know there is a sect out there that believes that athletic apparel is for kids, that once you are able to get your learner's permit you probably should stop walking around in that Dolphins jersey. This is not necessarily wrong; it's just too late. It's unenforceable. We are not going back to the old days of people in gray hats watching ballgames. It is not coming back. Don Draper is not taking you to the Yankees. Don Draper's grandson, Booger Draper, is, and he's wearing a Jorge Posada jersey.

★ Booger Draper is a great name for a band.

★ In my early twenties I went through a T-shirt-and-vest period. I don't mean a sweater vest. I mean a black cotton vest, with a T-shirt under it, sometimes worn with shorts and boots. I looked like Blossom hiking on the Appalachian Trail.

★ What is enraging about these periods in your life is, nobody says anything to you. They don't say anything because it's not polite, of course, but maybe we should say things. I would have really liked it if someone had pulled me aside and told me to stop wearing the black cotton vest and saved me from about three dozen really embarrassing photographs I cannot hang on the wall.

★ I also had a green cotton vest. I had two cotton vests. Seriously, why didn't somebody say something?

★ I once interviewed Tom Ford for a magazine story, and I put a lot of anxiety into what I'd wear that day—I'd brought my good suit, my good shirt, my good tie, which looked great to me but probably looked to him like I'd gotten dressed outside his office in the back of a van. Packing at the last minute, I'd rushed and thrown in a pair of novelty socks I'd gotten at Christmas. They were socks that had the days of the week written on them. And in the middle of this very serious interview, with arguably one of the most important voices in global fashion, a man so impeccable he looks like an Academy Award statue, Tom Ford looks at me and says, "What day is your sock?" I had no idea what he was talking about until I thought, *Oh dear*. Worse: the sock said THURSDAY. It was Wednesday.

★ You're in Tokyo," Tom Ford said. "It's Thursday in Tokyo."

★ I have not worn the day-of-the-week socks since.

★ To this point: avoid any "special" item. If you have a special tie or special socks or a special hat, there is somewhere between a 100 percent chance and a 100 percent chance that it is horrible. Nobody's special socks are black. Nobody's special tie is a simple knit navy-blue tie. The favorite socks have days of the week on them or chili lights wrapped around a statue of Mr. Spock. A favorite tie has a map of Las Vegas and a burlesque dancer on the back. Favorites are gifts to be worn the moment they are opened and then hidden in a drawer forever or hidden in the backyard under a foot of stone.

★ Your spouse already knows this, by the way. Your spouse has wanted to throw out your favorite hat since 1998.

★ I do not know if I am office-uniform material. In my life I have known several people who have embraced the office uniform: the idea of wearing basically the same exact thing to work every day. I read that the movie director Christopher Nolan goes with an office uniform. Mark Zuckerberg basically does. My old editor Peter went with navy blazer, plain-front khakis, Oxford shirt. It does simplify things. It seems less stressful. I once stayed at a house where I opened the closet and discovered that the owner had left a top row of jeans and a bottom row of black T-shirts. That was it! That is an unagonizing closet. After everyone realizes you're in the same outfit day in and day out, the novelty fades. When you do mix it up, it is a big deal. (When Peter wore an entire khaki suit, he looked like he was going to take an ocean liner to the Cannes Film Festival.) I just think I lack the discipline. I'd fail immediately. I'd do three days with the same T-shirt and jeans and a blazer and then I'd panic and wear a rabbit costume.

★ Things I can pull off:
  1. Sneakers with a suit.
  2. Tie bar.
  3. Toddler pizza vomit on T-shirt.

★ Things I cannot pull off:
  1. Jorts.
  2. Collarless shirts.
  3. Monocle.

★ *Act like you meant to do that.* Once I spent a day following around a celebrity stylist who dressed actors and actresses for the Oscars and bar mitzvahs and talk-show appearances and all that. We sat on a bench across from the Plaza Hotel on Fifth Avenue and watched the Manhattan crowd stroll by. It was early September, with enough of a crisp breeze that New Yorkers could finally surrender the flip-flops and resemble stylish humans, and it was fun and anthropological to sit with an expert and pay close attention to what people were wearing. This stylist offered a bit of advice that has always stuck, which was, whatever you do, look like you meant to do it. It is wise advice.

★ Looking like you meant to do it requires no cash or even expertise, just enough of a rush of confidence that whatever you are wearing, you intended. If your pants are six inches above the ankle, you meant to do that. If your dress has a rip down the side from accidentally bumping into the company snack machine, you meant to do that. Projection of confidence is 90 percent of the deal, the stylist assured me.

★ I know this doesn't excuse my cargo pants, but I don't care. I meant to do it.

Aunt Genie Says Mind Your Manners

One of my favorite people in the world is my wife's aunt, Genie. Like everybody else in my wife's oversized Baltimore family, Aunt Genie spends much of her summer enjoying the fresh air and scenery on a tiny island in the Saint Lawrence River, about a two-minute canoe ride from the Canadian border. My wife's family has been going to "the River" for nearly a century. It is a darling place, an archipelago of little rocky islands with cottages and wooden motorboats that look dreamt up for a children's book. It is also incredibly far away and hard to get to. It takes nearly eight hours to drive from New York City to the River by car, and in the seventh hour, because I am a jerk, I am prone to heaving a long, audible sigh and exclaiming, "We could have flown to *Denmark*!" When we finally arrive, we have to unload everything and take a boat. It is as if a hundred years ago my wife's forebears placed a wager on what would be the most arduous journey they could possibly take to relax on vacation and then blindfolded themselves until they made their way to an island in the Saint Lawrence they named Summerland. Yes, the island is called Summerland. I was not kidding about the children's book thing.

It takes so long to get to Summerland that by the time you go ashore, you need a drink. You need a few drinks. Here, the River is prepared. Almost always you can find Aunt Genie sitting on her porch dressed in something pink or green and possibly monogrammed, and if it's in the vicinity of 5:00 P.M., she's got you covered. I have spent many hours on that porch, admiring the view of the water and the gaggle of grandchildren playing on the docks, whining to anyone who will listen about the long drive, but mostly I listen to Aunt Genie. In Genie's family, she is the boss. Period. On her side of the island, all power flows down from her.

Aunt Genie embraces this part. She is in her eighth decade and has earned the right to tell people what to do. But I think what I like most about her is that she has a Way of Doing Things. She is a firm believer in etiquette—not strict, joyless rule-making, but the kind of manners and civility few people practice anymore. The moment you step onto Genie's porch, you start to behave yourself a little better. Kids in Genie's house do not pick up sofa cushions and fling them across the room—if they do, they will spend the night in the boathouse. Drinks are prompt, dinner is prompter, there's no yelling, no bickering, and hell no, your dog cannot come into her kitchen. Life has a comforting order to it. (My house, by contrast, feels as if a tribe of orangutans has gotten loose and opened up a case of Heinekens.)

I find Genie's house to be one of the more relaxing places on earth. "Etiquette" has become such a fading, antiquated term; it starts to sound like you're gnawing on hard candy or reading a newspaper in 1972. We have raised a planet to want what it wants when it wants it. Patience is in short supply. But good manners aren't an inconvenience—they're a relief, a survival strategy. The daily routine gets easier, less confrontational.

To be clear: it's essential to distinguish between manners and telling other people what to do. *Manners* is treating others with common courtesy and civility, the kind of behavior that people admire and want to emulate. *Telling other people what to do* is the kind of thing that gets you punched in the ear at Home Depot.

I feel a hundred years old saying this, but I worry about the erosion of those common courtesies. The impersonal nature of modern life has made rudeness easy. I'm as guilty as anyone— I've given the finger to so many drivers in the car that my kids probably think it's the left turn signal. But I do think my life could have a better order if I could just channel the civility at Aunt Genie's.

Here are some basic manners, courtesy of Aunt Genie. She's more direct than I am and is comfortable expressing her opinion about all this stuff. I just listened. We didn't have a cocktail when we talked, but we probably should have.

. . .

I figure it is helpful to start with <u>What the hell to do about thank-you notes</u>, since it is an essential yet dying etiquette art and nobody seems to have a straight answer on how to do it. Well, Aunt Genie knows. She thinks people who don't send prompt thank-you notes should be given light jail sentences. "Thank-you notes should be sent as soon as possible," she says. They should not be sent months later, as Bessie and I did after our wedding. (I honestly think we have, like, six more to send.) "Send them in a few days!" Genie barks. (See, I told you she had an opinion.) And don't listen to those weirdos who think it's impolite to mention the gift in a thank-you note. Genie says it's fine to mention the gift. That snow-cone maker you wouldn't use on a 200-degree day? Shower that snow-cone maker with love! "Explain how much you like the gift," Aunt Genie says. "Even if you don't." (Minor revelation here: Aunt Genie is cool with a minor white lie.)

★ <u>Can you e-mail a thank-you note?</u> I feel like I am asking Genie if I can build a Satanic temple in her backyard. "The old-fashioned thank-you note is better," she says politely. So don't be a slacker chump. Get a pen and a piece of paper; writing a handwritten thank-you note takes only one minute longer than microwaving a burrito. Your handwriting is not terrible. Wait, your handwriting is terrible. What is the matter with you?

★ <u>Can you send a text message as a thank-you note?</u> I think Aunt Genie might slap me across the face. She says only, "My mother would faint at the thought." (I am going to assume that Genie's mother did not have an iPhone 6.)

* <u>Invited to something? RSVP promptly. Come on.</u>
  "Leave a message and express your appreciation for being
  invited." Do not leave the host hanging for a couple of
  weeks while that opened invitation gets buried on the
  dining room table under a pile of Restoration Hardware
  catalogs.
* <u>"No Gifts" means what it says: no gifts.</u> If you're a socio-
  path who can't follow directions and simply *must* bring
  a gift, Aunt Genie recommends something small and
  eatable/drinkable—"a bottle of wine, something that can
  be consumed and has short-term value." So, not a puppy
  or a wayward child.
* <u>If you ask a host, "Is there anything I can bring?" and
  the host politely says, "Just bring yourself," bring flowers,</u>
  Aunt Genie says. See, here I had no idea. Yikes.
* <u>If you bring flowers, make sure they are in a vase</u> "so the
  host does not have to scramble around." When Aunt
  Genie tells me this, I realize I've been giving people
  flowers incorrectly for approximately twenty-three years.
  A vase? I have to carry a vase around with me? Thanks,
  Genie, this sounds like a huge pain in the ass.
* <u>Punctuality.</u> "So important for social engagements. Let's
  say you're having a dinner and you've invited everyone for
  seven o'clock and someone doesn't show until seven-thirty.
  It screws up when you're going to start dinner and how
  many cocktails you've served and it screws up the hostess."
  So, you don't want us there at sevenish?
* <u>Phones at the dinner table?</u> "No," Genie says. "Dreadful.
  Dreadful and not allowed at Thanksgiving or the cocktail

hour." This brings up another matter: I need to say "the cocktail hour" more in my life.

★ <u>Politics at the dinner table is absolutely forbidden</u>—"I don't have any objection to that. It makes for lively conversation." Especially if the cocktail hour has turned into cocktail three hours and fun Uncle Billy has some stuff to say about Bush/Gore 2000.

★ <u>Seating is the host's job.</u> I've made clear my aversion to assigned seating, but Aunt Genie's a believer. "You don't have to have place cards all over, but I think the host should have a seating plan written down to direct each person." Really? What about just winging it? "People are uncomfortable without a plan." Yes: next time I'm at Aunt Genie's for dinner, I am going to try to sit in someone else's seat, and will probably wind up kicked out and eating a turkey burger on the porch.

★ <u>Do not crowd-source a dinner menu.</u> "There are too many picky eaters," Genie says. It's true. Bessie and I are terrible dinner guests. My wife is a vegetarian who will eat fish; I am not a vegetarian, but I am allergic to fish. Basically, if you want to have us over to dinner, you have to serve sand.

★ <u>The host determines the dress code.</u> She might say, "I like men in jackets and ties for this special night." She might also say, "I don't give a damn." Genie is fine with either, but if you show up wearing a Phish shirt and Tevas, I think it's going to get a comment.

★ This etiquette conundrum has always driven me slightly insane: <u>When you are leaving a building, does the person</u>

<u>leaving hold the door for the person entering, or does the person entering hold the door for the person leaving?</u> It's the latter, Aunt Genie says. Hold the door for the person leaving! "Automatic!" she says. I feel this is our most-violated social rule on the planet, after spoiling TV shows.

★ <u>Shoes off in the house.</u> Genie actually doesn't care one way or the other; she just finds people taking off their shoes in the house amusing. Years ago a host never dreamed of telling people to take off their shoes. Do you think anybody told Eisenhower to take off his shoes when he walked inside the house? "Now all my grandchildren do it as soon as they walk in." She is laughing, but she is not complaining.

★ <u>What if someone you know has bad breath?</u> "You can't do anything about it unless it's a family member. But even then you can't do anything about it. Ignore it."

★ <u>What if you see a fly open?</u> "You have to know the person pretty well to say something. If I saw you with your fly open, I would tell Bessie to tell you the barn door is open. Ignore it if you don't know the person well. Sooner or later they will find out." I love that Genie says "the barn door is open."

★ <u>Crying baby in church?</u> "Get up and get the hell out of church."

★ <u>What is the polite thing to do if a stranger is sobbing uncontrollably next to you on an airplane?</u> "Oh, dear God."

★ <u>The pop-in visit to someone's house?</u> Nope. "Even if it's your own sister, it's more polite to let her know you are coming."

★ <u>When to leave a party.</u> "I believe that guests should all leave at once. But if you were the last guest, Jason, I wouldn't give a hoot. If I was tired, I'd just go to bed and say, 'See you tomorrow.'"

★ <u>Dogs in the house.</u> "Ugh. By permission only."

★ <u>What should I get my cat for its birthday?</u> "What? A cat? No."

Just before Thanksgiving 2014, Aunt Genie's husband, George, died after a long illness. George was a soft-spoken, lovely guy who once owned a hunting lodge in Colorado and rode bicycles and motorcycles into his eighties, and during those visits to the River, he and I had a zillion conversations about pedaling up mountain passes and the best rides up here near the Canadian border. Summers at the River will be different now. Or maybe not; Genie's family has been coming for generations, and the timelessness is much of the appeal.

If you ever get to Summerland, you can find me on Aunt Genie's porch, complaining about the eight-hour drive. The kids will be playing, the dogs will stay outside, and Aunt Genie will have the drinks. I'll bring flowers, finally with the vase.

And Here Are the Kids

We had a hard time. That's okay. A lot of people have a hard time. It's the cruel joke of wannabe parenthood: you spend your teenage years—probably your early twenties and maybe much more than that—nervous at the prospect of accidentally conceiving a child, and then, when you really want one, it proves to be agonizingly difficult. Like, it's at least ten times harder than finding a healthy salad at the airport. (That airport Cobb salad is not healthy—come on!)

If you are one of those people who was able to have a child immediately—all you had to do was think about children and there they were, hiding peanut butter crackers in the cracks of the sofa—congratulations. I salute your fertility and your fortune, and envy you. May you have eighteen children, enough to field your own World Series.

It was not that way for Bessie and me. We knew we wanted to have kids; there wasn't any hesitation about that. I had nothing left to add to the New York nightlife scene; by my mid-thirties, I was essentially a puttering ninety-nine-year-old man. For a while we tried the old-fashioned way, which is exciting—like removing the restrictor plates in a NASCAR race, which may or may not be the first time you've heard baby-making compared to NASCAR. But it wasn't working. It didn't work for so long that we decided to go to our doctors and solicit their professional medical opinions.

My man doctor worked in a second-floor office overlooking a park where people walked small dogs and fell asleep on benches after their morning methadone. He was tall and European and, like me, a huge cycling fan. We spent a little bit of time talking about my cancer history and a lot more time talking about the Tour de France. Lance Armstrong had just had a new child with a new girlfriend, which puzzled my doctor, who had been under the mistaken impression that chemo had rendered Armstrong sterile and he couldn't have any more kids.

"If you see him," he said, "you should find out how this is possible."

I told him I would see what I could do.

"Please ask," he said.

He called with my results a week later.

"Very low."

Say that again?

"You are not sterile, but you are very low," he said. "Very low. Your chances are basically—"

Yeah, yeah, I got it. The odds of Bessie and me conceiving naturally were around that of a Cleveland Browns Super Bowl. We were going to need help. I did have one bit of good fortune: that banked sperm. It was living in a little brownstone building on East 31st St. For many years I had sent a rent check to let my sperm live in a freezer without room service or HBO.

Bessie and I were about to enter the magical, wildly expensive, and often very frustrating world of fertility medicine. It was a three-year journey that would take us from a basement office on the upper Upper East Side of Manhattan to a "family center" in Brooklyn which felt as family-centered as a tire repair store, and finally to a clinic at New York University. Along the way there would be a lot of consultations, shots, pills, tests, failures, tears, and hours upon hours of loitering in waiting rooms. Parenthood was not assured. But I would read an astonishing number of *New Yorker*s and *Sports Illustrated*s.

I need to double-underline that this experience was approximately 100,000 times harder for Bessie than for me. She was the person absorbing the shots, taking the pills, making her confused body boil and rage. I just had to be the knucklehead with the needle. I took my knucklehead needle job seriously, however. When we began trying in vitro fertilization (IVF), there was a climactic shot called the hCG shot. The needle looked like something you'd use to put down a panther at the mall, and it had to be mixed together correctly and delivered at a very specific time. Bessie would lie down nervously in the living room and I'd sit over her—you may recall John Travolta hovering over Uma Thurman in *Pulp Fiction*—with Bessie begging me to count it down—5, 4, 3, 2, 1—before plunging in. One time I hit a vein and the needle shot back out, blood splattering over me. We both screamed, and I had to do the whole deal all over again—new needle, new shot, new 5, 4, 3, 2, 1.

Happens all the time, the nurse said later.

I kept telling myself that if these shots had to be delivered precisely and perfectly, there was no way they would give it to a knucklehead to try at home. But the process would stress us in ways we'd never been stressed. And it was exhausting and costly. It sounds tacky to talk about—how can you talk about money when potential parenthood is on the line?—but it's always a hurdle, in the back of your mind. How can it not be? Every IVF treatment costs about the price of a lightly used Honda. I don't want to talk specific amounts, but know that now I own several lightly used nonexistent Hondas.

A cruel razor of fertility treatment is that it's pass/fail. There is no moral victory. It works or it doesn't. There are, of course, people who get pregnant on the first try. We were not those people. We would raise our hopes, and it would crush us again and again. You begin to distrust the whole ritual. You turn away from science. One day I went into a religious gift store not far from our apartment, explained my situation, and bought candles. It was very comforting how seriously they took this request—as if lighting a candle to deliver a baby made perfect, rational sense. We lit the candles before every test we took. We were paying for the cutting edge, and we were down to the candles.

We got numb to the failures and began to close the door.

We couldn't admit that to each other—it was so raw and unthinkable—but we confronted the reality privately by ourselves. Some couples just don't get pregnant. It was okay. We began to consider other options, like adoption. This was a long and complicated process too, but it could be just as rewarding.

In the lowest times, we realized how much we wanted this. The ambivalence that had lingered into our thirties was long gone. It got hard to walk around the neighborhood—we'd walk 100 yards to the bakery and pass a dozen happy couples pushing strollers, and it was quietly heartbreaking.

Exhausted with IVF, ready to move on, we went in for one last try. One final, beautiful, hopeful lightly used Honda. It was shortly on the heels of a failed attempt, and frankly, this time we just went through the motions. There was none of the intensity of before. No 5, 4, 3, 2, 1. Just get it done, Bessie would say, lying on the couch.

We knew better than to get our hopes up. And we were in the car on our way to what we thought would be the world's loneliest couple's vacation when we got a call from the doctor's office. Bessie was afraid to pick up the phone. She'd had enough bad news from that number. When she picked up, she listened for a moment and then gasped. She put her phone on speaker and asked the nurse to say it again.

You are pregnant.

Say it again.

Pregnant.

And then we both started to cry.

It is more than three years later and Jesse is here and so

is Josie—also an IVF production, this time considerably less stressful—and yes, we have lost all perspective from those low moments. We get overwhelmed and frustrated with our kids like anyone else. We chase Jesse in the store, we struggle when he hurls his breakfast on the floor, we shake our heads when he throws a screaming tantrum because we won't let him drink the water in the humidifier. It's not like we say, *Well, Jesse, we were considering giving you a time-out, but we remember full well the nights when we lost all those embryos and we never thought you were possible*. Nah. It's still hard, exhausting, and the peanut butter crackers in the sofa are no joke.

When the kids are asleep? That's when I feel it. I'll be walking down the hallway to our bedroom and I'll have my mind on something dumb like a basketball score or some nonsense from work and I will pass their little room. For a long time it was this sad unused room that we never were quite sure what to do with. Is it an office? A guest room? A storage room for unnecessary crap? I used to ride a stationary bike in that room. That was never what that room was for.

That's going to be the baby's room, we would say. But there were a lot of long gray months and years when it belonged to nobody.

Now it's getting late, and as I pass by, I sense the kids, new and thrilling, still a joyful mystery.

That room belongs to somebody.

That's when I know how fortunate we are.

. . .

★ Yes! We are in our early days here. Chapter One. Maybe Chapter One and a Half. We haven't even got the car out of the driveway. If you are a parent of vast experience, you are permitted to laugh at me here. I know you are laughing at me. You look upon me with a mixture of pity and wonder: *You really have no idea.* And it's true: I have no idea. Well, I have some idea, but not enough of an idea to consider myself anywhere close to an authority. My brother, whose daughter is on the verge of her teens, treats me like I'm still in the first season of *Breaking Bad. Wait until Season 4*, he says, *when it takes your kid two hours to dress before school.* And of course there are parents with kids older than his kid who are warning him about high school and boyfriends and Snapchat. That's the thing about being a parent: there's always somebody a little bit further down the path, chuckling about your impending doom. You can be the parents of a fifty-eight-year-old, and parents of sixty-year-olds will be like, *Oh, man, fifty-eight is a walk in the park compared to sixty! Wait until your sixty-year-old steals your back brace.*

★ I'm scared by this new era of hyperjudgmental overparenting—you're supposed to raise children this way, not that way, and in French or Mandarin, and organic-only, farm-to-table, gender-neutral, pasteurized—or is it unpasteurized? I'm not sure. Fresh advice arrives almost daily, unsolicited. Your child is not supposed to have soda or sugar or pants that contain polyester fibers until he or she is thirty-seven. You should be enrolling in prekindergarten in the second trimester and Swedish summer camp in the third trimester. By ten months the child should be able to walk, subscribe to the *New York Review of Books*, and play the oboe. If your children cannot do these things, they will wind up a stowaway on a barge. New York is abundant with this kind of obsessive parenting culture—it gets amplified by magazines and newspapers, which love nothing better than to prey upon the insecurities of new moms and dads, who then become paranoid that they're failing if their four-year-old can't name all the justices on the Supreme Court or pronounce "mise-en-scène."

★ I refuse to join this ridiculousness. There are plenty of things I worry about with my kids—I hope they stay healthy; I want them to go outside and run around as much as possible; I am terrified they'll become Jets fans, and I will move my family to the Maldives to prevent it— but parenting has made me a lot less judgmental. I have no idea what *I'm* doing. Who am I to judge? I empathize with any mom or dad trying to have an honest go at the job. Unshaven dad chasing his kids in Whole Foods while wearing sweatpants and Crocs? I feel I know you. I *am* you. When I see a parent trying to alleviate a child's tantrum, all I think is, *That could be MY child's tantrum, and no offense, but I am very happy it is instead YOUR child's tantrum.* I have no urge to give that parent unsolicited advice. I want to give that parent a beer. Or three beers.

★ All the time you hear people say, "Oh so-and-so, she makes parenting look so easy." And I think here the operative word is "look." There are people who are capable of making parenting look graceful, even glamorous or stylish, and of course there are people fortunate enough to have armies of nannies and tennis coaches and baby stylists (what, you don't have a baby stylist?). But mostly I think easy parenting is a mirage. Parenting is brutal at times for everybody. The nerves fray for everyone. The handbook becomes useless. Improvisation takes over. When it starts to go sideways, I find it helpful to imagine I'm in a Marx Brothers movie in which nothing will ever go according to plan. You will bathe your child, dress your child, get your child fully ready to go out the door on a cold winter morning—it's like preparing a 201-year-old man for a space walk—and right as you are ready to step out that door, he will squeeze a tube of yogurt on his head. And then you have to undo everything and start all over again. I've learned to embrace this randomness, because it's not random at all. It's the gig.

★ Your own parents, of course, are a reservoir of extremely useful and slightly dated parenting advice. Raising you was almost surely a very different experience for your parents. They were probably younger, fitter, more energetic. Back then, in olden days, parenting was less expensive, less obsessive, less manic. Your mother was not Googling ergonomic baby shoes at 2:00 A.M. Being a new mom or dad was viewed as a normal human passage, not extraordinary life theater. Parents back then smoked, let their kids sleep on their stomachs, ride in the front of the car. My brother and I always tell ourselves our parents had it easy. *All Mom and Dad had to do was dump us out into the yard!*

When they wanted us to come home, they just yelled from the back porch! We took care of ourselves! This is partly true but mostly our own inane foggy recollection. Of course it was hard. Of course it was anxious. Years have a way of sanding off the rough edges and softening the hard times. My mom talks about us having chicken pox as if it were some hilarious cocktail party she went to.

★ Grandparenting is quite a different deal from parenting. It's the difference between being a journeyman starter and a well-paid left-handed relief pitcher. At this point in her life, my mom is not going to come down and take care of the kids for three weeks. Nana can come in and face two batters. Jesse and Josie love it. I love it too. But there are some helpful guidelines. Early on, my brother offered this advice: When you entrust the child to a grandparent, you have to relinquish all control. And this means everything. You can't worry about Grandma or Grandpa doing it the way you do it. Grandma may *attempt* to find organic crackers at the truck stop, but if those don't work, it's straight to the sour cream and onion Pringles. Grandma might not let the toddler watch more than ten minutes of TV, or she might let him watch *There's Something About Mary* in its entirety. It's okay. If you don't want your kid to eat Oreos for a midnight snack, don't give your kid a grandparent.

★ People will tell you that parenthood is a leveler, and that is true. It is common ground between you and people who in no way resemble you. I have discussed parenthood with my mother and my mother-in-law and with Guy, my wise, cigar-smoking neighbor, and, because of my job, with Roger Federer and Beyoncé (the latter as Beyoncé's baby, Blue, cried in the background). Beyoncé's bodyguard even recommended a stroller to me. Well, maybe I shouldn't say he *recommended* it, but he really talked that thing up. It was curvy and tall and resembled a hotel in Dubai. I went home and told my wife that we should get this stroller because Beyoncé's bodyguard had recommended it, and she looked at me as if I were wearing a Big Bird costume. I had visions of pushing this stroller around the neighborhood, and when we invariably got into conversations about the relative merits of contemporary baby strollers, I would mention—casually, of course—that we'd purchased this stroller on the recommendation of Beyoncé's bodyguard. After a few weeks I would have probably just shortened "Beyoncé's bodyguard" to "Beyoncé."

★ We did not get that stroller. It cost about $1,000 and weighed as much as a grizzly bear.

★ I live in a neighborhood infested with children—they're crawling out of the cracks in the sidewalk, demanding vegan ice cream sandwiches—and every once in a while there's a revolt: a neighborhood bar, frustrated with $8 tabs and picking up chewed popcorn from the floor, gets huffy and declares that kids aren't welcome anymore. I understand the backlash. If I am twenty-four and having twenty-four-year-old cool times, I do not want to look over at a bunch of flabby dads sharing pretzels with their toddlers and asking them if they "made a stinky." But is this really an epidemic? Can't everyone time-share the bar? Let's be clear: nothing that thrilling ever happens in a bar before nine o'clock. By then kids—and their parents—are long gone. If you are single and in a bar at 3:45 P.M. you have bigger issues than my kid coloring a Dr. Seuss coloring book next to you. Also, please pass the crayons.

★ Before I had children, I was always mystified by a classic, perennial human-interest story: the pesky toddler who somehow manages to wedge him- or herself inside a crane game at the arcade. You know the kind of game I am talking about: those games in which you put in fifty cents and try to move a flimsy metal crane around and pick up a candy bar or a rainbow-colored bear worth about eight and a half cents. Every now and again a small child somewhere somehow wedges himself or herself up through the delivery chute and crawls into the game, suddenly trapped behind glass, amid the bears and candy bars. It happens surprisingly often, and it's the kind of story local news stations and the Internet go bonkers about. And I used to think, *How the* hell *did that happen? What is* wrong *with that child's parents?* Today, as a parent, I can *totally* see how it happens. My toddler's main ambition in life is to get into things he's not supposed to get into. He sees that arcade machine as a glorious challenge. *Nothing* would make him happier than getting inside it. It's a wonder it doesn't happen more. This is the essence of parenting, right? Stop your kid from getting into the crane game.

★ At the moment we are in the "can't go out to dinner" portion of parenthood. The baby, Josie, is easy—you can take a baby to a three-star Michelin restaurant and drop a champagne bottle on the floor, and that lump will just lie there in a basket and snooze away. Toddlers, nope—no way. With Jesse we try to get away with it—enough time passes that we think, *Okay, maybe we can pull it off*—but taking him out to eat is like walking into a dining room and opening a mesh bag full of vampire bats. Chaos instantly. We make adjustments: we feed him a little before, we order before we sit, we ask for the check to come before the entrées. Doesn't matter. Within moments he is running around the restaurant, taking his fork to strangers' meals.

★ My wife and I have occasional gentle disagreements about food. My wife is adamant about giving the child the best food—organic only, if possible, avoiding the processed junk and fast food that is a staple of the American diet. I agree with this mission 100 percent. I also believe the child can have a hot dog without turning into a serial killer. (Not a street-cart hot dog. Don't be crazy—those *completely* turn you into a serial killer.) I also plan one day to open a chain of kid-friendly restaurants called Family Trough, in which the whole clan can eat soup, nachos, and whole apples facedown in a rectangular trough you can take home with you if you don't finish.

★ *Embrace the hand-me-down.* Before we had kids, I had an aversion to the idea of hand-me-downs. I was too focused

on the *me-down* part. I obnoxiously thought Jesse's fashion
style needed to be built from the ground up, with no prior
influences and certainly no pre-barfed-upon Ramones
T-shirts. My wife wisely overruled my stupidity and col-
lected as many hand-me-downs as possible. I realized this
was the proper move within forty-eight hours of Jesse's
birth. When you see the exciting materials that come out
of a small child, you realize you don't want to own any
piece of clothing that costs more than a hot pretzel.

★ Of course, in a moment of affection you may vacate your
senses and buy insane fashion wear for your kid. Not long
after Jesse was born, we bought him a pair of jeans that I
think cost more than my rent did in college. It was waste-
ful and mortifying, and I'm turning red as I type this. But
you had to see these jeans. Cute little French shop (of
course) in Manhattan (of course), and my wife and I were
having one of those weekend walks in which our family
felt the way families look in Tommy Hilfiger ads. Jesse was
being such a good boy, so much that we wanted to reward
him, which he didn't ask for or need, of course, but it was
this perfect autumn day, and when we walked into the
French baby clothes store, Bessie saw this adorable pair of
jeans that could fit nicely on Kermit the Frog. The price
was more than either of us had ever spent on jeans, for
ourselves, as *adults*, and surely we could have walked up
the street, like, two blocks and found baby jeans that were
basically 97 percent as good for, say, ten bucks. (I feel like
I am confessing to a murder.) And now Bessie is seeing the

ridiculousness of it, saying, "This is too much to spend" and folding up the adorable baby jeans, but suddenly I am bolting past her and throwing down the credit card for those jeans. And they turned out to be pretty adorable. I regret nothing.

★ I have no idea where those jeans are now.

★ Not long ago I took Jesse to see some of my old bike friends at a bike race. I was carrying him around and I ran into my friend Kenny, who is in his fifties and one of the better bike racers in town. The last of Kenny's kids had just graduated from college—someplace fancy, like Dartmouth. The kids were out of the house. The crazy parenting highway that I just started on was suddenly wide open to Kenny. He could do just whatever. On weekends he could sleep until ten. He could just linger in restaurants for hours upon hours. He could go on bike rides twice a day. But when Kenny saw me with Jesse, he walked up and asked, "Can I hold him for a second?" He took Jesse and his twenty-five or so pounds and he pressed him close and gave him this long hug and brushed a hand through his hair. I thought Kenny was going to tear up. And after a while he said, "You know how much I have missed this? You have *no* idea how you are going to miss that one day."

★ It was beautiful. And yes, I was hoping that Jesse would poop so we could find out how much Kenny missed *that*.

Epilogue: Come Over Right Now

Dad was on his way out. This we knew. My brother Chris and I had been alternating in shifts at the hospital, and I was back at my parents' house when he sent a text we'd all been expecting: *You should come in now.*

I called a taxi, and it showed up faster than a taxi had ever shown up in the history of taxis, and I explained the situation to the driver, and he really stiffened in his seat and rose to the occasion, or at least his right foot did, all business, autobahnning it up Route 2 to Storrow Drive along the Charles River and up to Mass General in a matter of . . . it was minutes, the fastest I'd ever gotten to that part of town in my life. I jumped out while the car was still basically moving and then *push push pushed* at the elevator button and up to the ninth floor, where we had all spent most of the last couple of weeks. I rushed past the lobby with the old magazines I'd read cover to cover and around the corner desk area where the nurses sat and toward my father's room at the end of the corridor. My mom was on the phone to her sister, and Chris was at Dad's bedside and my dad was . . .

Well, Dad was dead.

He'd been dead for some time, my brother said. Maybe a half hour.

"But fifteen minutes ago you texted, 'You should come in now,'" I said.

"Right," he said.

"And he was dead?"

"Yes."

"I think 'You should come in now' means you should come in *now* because Dad is *about* to die," I said. "Not 'You should come in *now* because Dad is *dead*.'"

"What difference does it make?"

"'You should come in now' means *still alive*."

"'Come in now' means come in now. What: am I supposed to tell you to stay home?"

"'Come in now' means hanging by a thread, like there's still time."

"Hmmm. I am not sure about that."

We sounded like Jerry and George bickering in the kitchen on *Seinfeld*.

Meanwhile there was Dad, poor Dad, ravaged, pale, gone, tucked hard into the bed. The truth was he'd slipped away quietly, before Chris or my mom had much of a chance to notice.

There had been no drama, no final words, no last-second revelation of a stash of gold buried underneath the garage. Nurses and doctors had come by for hugs and quiet conversations, but all it felt like was the inevitable, which is what it had felt like for a while.

When you lose a loved one, they say it doesn't hit you immediately but sneaks up on you quietly, at a distance. In the days and weeks and months after Dad died, I kept waiting for it to sneak up. I got through his funeral fine—eight-minute eulogy, packed church, Mom in the front row, got some laughs, didn't cry. I didn't cry at the party afterward or on the drive home or even during a final look into his closet, the rows of cotton sweatshirts labeled *Coach*. I wore one of his old gray sweatshirts around for months. Nothing.

Father and son is a complicated relationship, certainly by nature, probably by design—so much is given and expected, to the point that it's hard to live up to any of it. The relationship is almost all emotion—no professional distance, little perspective. My dad, like almost every dad, had his episodes as mentor, adversary, advocate, and tyrant. He could be thoughtful and tender but also fly off the handle unnecessarily, cartoonishly, freak out when freaking out was not the right thing. I spent way too much time being ungrateful and mad. We argued into my adulthood. As I got older, it got better. Parenthood softened me; grandparenthood softened him. Plus he was good at it—a full-on, babbling, googly-woogly granddad, sticking a tennis racket in Jesse's hand before he could crawl, showing Jesse the same summer constellations he showed me when I was Jesse's age. Nothing makes you love a parent more than seeing their love for your own kid.

His goodbye had been so quick. Less than six months, when it was all said and done, March to August. It had been too fast to engineer an ideal exit. Before he'd gotten sick, I'd been developing a semi–bucket list for him, Things I Wanted to Do with Dad Before He Croaked, and it included the golf Masters and Wimbledon in England. I'd already begun to offer, and he'd declined. We had time. Maybe next year. In April, right after he was diagnosed, I made a final push for the Masters. One morning I was talking to some scalpers outside Augusta National Golf Club, and I called Dad right then, told him I'd priced it out, I'd take care of it, just get on the plane, he just had to see this once. I hoped he'd say to hell with it and get on a plane. He could not. He did not.

This is the part where I beg: don't wait.

His daily life narrowed to modest accomplishments. That summertime trip to the restaurant with my mother. A walk around the block. A conversation with his grandkids. Everything about his grandkids. He found time to dote on Bessie, who was pregnant with Josie, a grandkid he'd never meet. There were mornings that he was animated enough to become angry about the Red Sox. The ability to be mad about something meaningless made him happy.

A couple nights before Dad died, Chris had his daughter, Blue, and Blue's mom, Violaine, up to visit the hospital, and at some point I suggested they try to get Red Sox tickets. Blue had never gone to Fenway Park. I was adamant: *Aww, ya gotta take the kid to Fenway!* Somehow Chris managed to wrangle primo tickets right next to the Boston dugout. That night I turned on the game in Dad's hospital room, and we discovered that every time the TV cameras flashed to a left-handed batter—*Hey, it's Big Papi!*—you could see Chris, Blue, and Vio sitting there on the baseline, huddled like penguins. Dad was so medicated I wouldn't have blamed him if he thought he was hallucinating. But he noticed, and it made him smile.

Later in the evening he asked me to help him adjust his bed. I have been in plenty of hospitals, and I have never been able to figure out the beds. They have dashboards that look like those in Russian space shuttles, and it is a law of the universe that you must fling the controls in three different incorrect directions before you finally get where you are going to go. Dad wanted to sit up a little bit, and I went over to the left side of the bed, leaned over, and pressed . . . aw, crap, wrong button.

"NOOOOOOO!" he howled, furiously fixing me in the eyes. "WHAT ARE YOU? THE FUUUUU—"

He so clearly was about to say "The fuck are you doing?" but he held up, maybe out of politeness but probably out of exhaustion. He just looked at me. I felt like I was back taking my driver's test at sixteen, when the state driving examiner announced that he was passing me even though I missed a few turns and my dad, sitting in the back seat, tried to argue that he should flunk me.

Dad's yelling didn't make me upset. It thrilled me. It was a signal of life. I found the proper button, and the bed whizzed and hummed, and he sank back down to prone level.

It would be our last interaction. The next day Dad drifted in and out of consciousness. He managed to say some nice things about my mother—sweet and grateful things she deserved, after all she'd done to help him—but mostly he was out of it. At one point he looked close to slipping away and I asked if he was seeing anything. Light, gates, heavenly anything? A Dunkin' Donuts in the sky! Borg-McEnroe 1980! He'd loved to fish—did he see a striped bass run in Montauk?

"What are you doing?" Chris asked me.

"You never really know!" I said.

My brother rolled his eyes. "You're insane," he said.

The next morning Dad was gone.

A month later I wondered if I was ever going to feel it. People came up to me and said nice things about my father, and I appreciated all of it, from his students and his tennis players and his colleagues at school. But it didn't break me down. I wrote a tribute to him in the *Journal* and I approached it as if I were writing about somebody I wasn't related to, interviewing his former students and players, trying to render a realistic person.

Months passed. For a few winters, I'd been playing in a goofy indoor adult tennis league near my house with a bunch of other flabby hackers who thought they were still reasonably good at the game. I had developed a ritual of calling my father from the car on the way home for a postmatch assessment— I'd give him the score, tell him how it had gone, describe my opponent's style, and analyze my approach. Even if the match ended late at night, he'd stay up back in Massachusetts, waiting for the call.

These were some of my favorite conversations I ever had with my dad. We talked about successes and mistakes, the lessons I'd learned, the things I'd do differently the next time. They were not big things. Small steps. Marginal improvements.

That December I played my first league match, and I got thumped, really thumped, the kind of loss that makes you want to take your tennis racket and puree it in a blender. I had no answers for the kind of player I usually beat easily, and the whole match was over a lot sooner than it should have been. It was around 11:00 P.M. as I got to the car, and when I sat inside and turned it on, I reached for the button on the dashboard. It was time to call Dad. His number popped up on the screen, and the phone began to dial.

I'd forgotten.

And I hung up the call and began to cry, and I cried for a really long time, in a way that felt like I could begin to move forward.

I'm going to make so many mistakes, but I know it is okay. I'll take the small steps. Marginal improvements.

Little victories.

Acknowledgments

I wrote this book during a crazy year in my family's life—some of which was very sad, but most of which was life-affirming, even the parts stuck on the New Jersey Turnpike.

I'm grateful to many people for help along the way.

Thank you to Bill Thomas, who guided this project with wisdom and patience, which is remarkable, since Bill is a fan of the New York Yankees. The great David McCormick was nutty enough to think this book was a good idea, but David also thinks a golf vacation is a good idea. I am grateful to Rose Courteau and Emma Borges-Scott, as well as the relentless Todd Doughty. Thank you to John Vilanova for your input and careful eye. Thanks also to Nick Khan, Michael Davies, Sarah Aubrey, Alissa Bachner, Pete Berg, and everyone at Film 44.

At the *Wall Street Journal*: Thank you to Sam Walker and Mike Miller for being daft enough to hire me, and thank you to my encouraging overlords Robert Thomson and Gerry Baker for not canning Sam and Mike for hiring me. Thanks also to editors Darren Everson, Jim Chairusmi, Geoff Foster, Derick Gonzalez, Kevin Helliker, and Matt Oshinsky for their guidance and making sure I don't misspell "Nowitzki." That is how you spell "Nowitzki," isn't it?

A huge thanks to *WSJ* readers everywhere. You all completely rock.

I am grateful for mentors of all types: Dick and Jody Reston at the *Vineyard Gazette*; Gareth Cook and Peter Kadzis at the *Boston Phoenix*; my *GQ* and ex-*GQ* friends Jim Nelson, Devin Friedman, Mark Healy, Andy Ward, Michael Hainey, Fred Woodward, Mary Stiehl, and Adam Rapoport. At *Vogue* I am indebted to Anna Wintour, Eve MacSweeney, Taylor Antrim, Jill Demling, and of course, Beyoncé.

Peter Kaplan brought me to New York City. I miss him every single day.

I feel like an orchestra is going to play me off at any second—Thanks to Chris Gay, Violaine Etienne, Blue Etienne-Gay, the Reckers, Ali Tenenbaum, Dan/Josh/BR/V/Dicky, Rob Lombardi, Alessandro Matteucci, and all of the NYC peloton. Thanks to Philip and Wilson Kerr, Dom & Jamie, Scocca, Crowley, the late shift at Rodrick Industries, Inc., Omar at the mail shop, and Bar Bruno. Thanks to the Maturines—Osheal, Nikita, and Mr. Thez. A huge thank you to Bob Oster, Ann Oster, Nick Oster, Erin Hall, and Lori Mulligan, and of course to the amazing, impeccable Genie Flinn for her sharp advice. Thank you to all my in-laws from Baltimore and Summerland. I'd name you, but if I forgot one of you, I'd be booted off the island.

Okay, cousin Hunter, you owe me $1.

Thanks to my mom, Marilyn Gay, for everything—you're a remarkable person, a globe-trotter, an inspiration, the glue. And thank you to my father, Ward Gay, who played a brilliant five-setter (no tiebreakers) until the end. I miss him very much.

My family is very grateful to everyone who was there for us during my father's final months.

Thanks to my children, Jesse and Josie, who can't read this yet, and probably need to start cracking.

Finally, thank you to Bessie Oster: my partner, friend, canoe boss, role model, and loveliest person I know. Also: definitely the only person I know who once left home and joined the circus. For real.

I love you all.

ABOUT THE AUTHOR

Jason Gay is a sports columnist at *The Wall Street Journal* and the MVP of Super Bowl XLIX.[1] He has written for publications including *Vogue*, *GQ*, *Rolling Stone*, and the *New York Observer*. He lives in Brooklyn with his family and a passive-aggressive cat.

---

[1] Okay, fine. Tom Brady was the MVP of Super Bowl XLIX.